VACATIONING
with
GOD

JACK LIN

Vacationing with God
©2021 Jack Lin

All rights reserved. No part of this publication may be reproduced, distributed, or transmitted in any form or by any means, including photocopying, recording, or other electronic or mechanical methods, without the prior written permission of the publisher, except in the case brief quotations embodied in critical reviews and other noncommercial uses permitted by copyright law.

ISBN:
Paperback   978-1-63945-125-8
E-book   978-1-63945-126-5

The views expressed in this book are solely those of the author and do not necessarily reflect the views of the publisher, and the publisher hereby disclaims any responsibility for them.

Writers' Branding
1800-608-6550
www.writersbranding.com
orders@writersbranding.com

CONTENTS

Introduction xi
Introduction 2 xiii
Foreword xv

Part I Adventures

Chapter One: Arrival To The Holy Land
    Sometimes We Must Travel Far To Find Ourselves 1
    Adventure One - The Nativity/Christian For A Day 4
    Adventure Two - Visiting Hebron 8
    Adventure Three - Visiting Rachel's Tomb 13

Chapter Two: Spiritual Experiences
    The Non-Rational Part Of Life - The Numinous Experience 19

Chapter Three: Resting Places
    Adventure Four – Tombs Ofncients – Northern Israel 23
    Adventure Five - The Tomb Of Absalom 26

Chapter Fou: Spiritual Places
    Wrestling With God 33

Chapter Five: Walls And Wells
    Drinking Holy Water 37
    Adventure Six - Mary's Well In Nazareth 37
    Adventure Seven – The Western Wall 40

Chapter Six: The Trip To Mount Sinai
    Adventure Eight (A) – Climbing Mount Sinai.................................. 52
    Adventure Eight (B) – The Call To 54
    Prayer (The Adhan) Muslim For A Day... 54

Chapter Seven: The Power Of Stone
    Adventure Nine – King David's Tomb.. 63
    Adventure Ten – The Wall Again.. 67

Chapter Eight: Church Of The Holy Sepulcher
    Adventure Eleven - Christian For A Day... 71

Chapter Nine: Mount Moriah And The Dome Of The Rock
    Touching The Starting Point Of Western Religions 79
    Adventure Twelve - Dome Of The Rock.. 81

Part II: Reflections And Analysis Of Israel

Chapter Ten: Historical Civilizations
    God Touching The Past Cultures.. 93

Chapter Eleven: The Jewish Civilization
    God Touching Man – The Past.. 103
    Miracle 1... 109

Chapter Twelve: Part A Miracles
    God Touching Man – The Present.. 111
    Miracles 2 – 12... 111
    Miracle 2... 112
    Miracle 3... 113
    United States Miracle 4 115
    United States Miracle 5 115
    United States Miracle 6 116
    Miracle 7... 123
    Miracle 8... 125
    Miracle 9... 126
    Miracle 10... 126

Miracle 11 127
Miracle 12 128

Chapter Twelve: Part B Miracles
  Man Touching God - The Past 133

Chapter Twelve: Part C
  12 - Part C - The Future 143

Afterword 145
Appendix 151
Endnotes 155

"The highest point a man can attain is not Knowledge, or Virtue, or Goodness, or Victory, but something even greater, more heroic and more despairing: Sacred Awe!"

- Nikos Kazantzakis

*Dedicated to
Dr. Brueh Joy
"Vivere deinde Philosophare"
"Live, then philosophize"
(Carl Jung)*

Editor – Sheri Lin, MA

The Jewish National Fund helped supply the photos in this book.

INTRODUCTION

This book is an invitation to do something that you and I have probably urged others to do, but rarely do ourselves: Be open to new experiences. How often have you heard this or said it to yourself? As a professor, I have said it a hundred times, but have only done it a few times in my life. Fortunately, one of the times is when I read and absorbed this book of experiences and adventures by Jack Lin.

I suspect that many of us have had an experience that we would call being in touch with the Deity. I also suspect that most of us have been reluctant to admit to others that we have had such feelings. Perhaps this is because we are in an age of science and technology and such feelings don't seem quite in touch with the times.

I think that many more of us would like to feel in touch with something beyond everyday experiences and feelings. This book is a kind of guide and source for those among us who would like to be more in touch with their spiritual feelings. You might want to just let yourself go and join the author as he travels around the world and allows himself to acknowledge and experience the Deity.

I would also urge you to not put off such experiences until you are in the same places as the author. I don't think it is always necessary to be in a specific place to have such experiences. You should not deny yourself any opportunities because you are in more ordinary places.

Israel is the Homeland to three of the major Western Religions and their history is there. However, on this vacation don't seek the religious doctrine. Religion asks you to believe what you have been told, but these laws, traditions, stories, etc., are the remembrance of the original Mystics who experienced them. On this vacation, the author asks you to find your own mystical experiences.

The experiences and adventures that the author and others have encountered in this book, may not follow their own religious dogma. Spiritual experiences are so deep and so real, it effects the individual with a feeling of joy, peace and ecstasy, and in fact, it is ineffable. If you immerse yourself in the Holy soul of God, you may feel ecstasy and this experience may change your life.

Ecstasy is an interesting word. In fact, there is a synthetic drug that young people use today called Ecstasy. The short pharmaceutical name for it is MDMA, a drug that alters your mood and perception. Ecstasy is a trans-like state, in which an individual transcends normal consciousness. Unfortunately, if you use the synthetic drug to achieve the "state of ecstasy" the effect can be either dark or bright. It can also be addictive.

When you experience ecstasy through a spiritual experience, there is no baggage, ill-effects or problems that can come with it. It is an overpowering emotion and exaltation and opening awareness of the universe and God.

Join hands with the author and other adventurers in this book and discover your own soul!

Two thousand years ago, Rabbi Hillel asked: "If I am not for myself, who will be for me? If not now, when?"

If not now, when will you open yourself up to experiences the Divine?
Professor - Dr. George Zilbergeld

INTRODUCTION 2

The Talmud tells a story of a man who wandered in the desert, weary, hungry and thirsty. He came upon a tree with sweet fruit, a pleasant shade and stream of water flowing beneath it. He ate from its fruit, drank from its water and relaxed in its shade. As he was about to depart, a refreshed traveler, he turned to the tree and said, "Tree, oh tree, how can I bless you? Shall I bless you, that your fruit shall be sweet? They are already so! Shall I bless you with pleasant shade? You already have it! Shall I bless you that a stream of water pass beneath you? One already does! All I can bless you with is that the trees that are offspring of you shall be like you."

Dr. Jack Lin embodies the verse in Psalms "They search for God where he can be found, where He is close to Him." As a man of science and history, he was hungry for substantive truth, so he traveled to Israel to see, feel, hear, touch and smell God's footprints here on earth. As a man of enlightenment, he was thirsty for spirituality, so he traveled to places of major spiritual events connected to God's omnipresence. As a man of psychology, he was curious, so he searched his conscious and subconscious worlds to discover an inner omnipotence.

Over the last six months that I have known the author, I have learned that he no longer the wanderer of this parable, but has become the tree. His fruits of philanthropy have forever improved Jewish life in Israel, our homeland. His shade of protection hovers wide above his beloved friends and family. His curiosity flows like a river, constantly moving forward towards far reaching discovery. There is much to learn and emulate from this man of youth, sincerity and abundance.

JACK LIN

To all the young people out there that are still unsure of their passion, dreams and inner truth: deep down, we're all weary, hungry and thirsty. That is a good thing! When harnessed, these characteristics propel us to become energetic, sustained and brimming with achievement. Spend some time with Dr. Jack, and you'll see why.

In this book, the author shares many experiences and discoveries that fall outside of my area of experience. Jewish law prohibits the study of the nation's deities. This ruling precludes my ability to read, recommend or comment on those aspects, events and discussions.

Man's search for meaning will never end. The author will be the first to tell you that when you spend time, "Vacationing with God", there will always be time for one more week. Each moment of "Vacationing with God", is packed with potential. This book contains some powerful stories of the Jewish ancient holy sites. The message of hope you can take away, is that God is very close to us and always will be. As it states in Deuteronomy, "Not in the heavens… and not beneath the surface of the earth, not across the ocean, is it… for the matter is very close to you, in your mouth and in your heart, that you may achieve it".

Rabbi Isser Kluwgant
CEO and Spiritual Mentor
Chabad at Pierce
Woodland Hills, CA

FOREWORD

If you wish to travel to a remarkable place and discover yourself, I strongly suggest you visit a sacred land, where you can find your soul regardless of your religious affiliation, or even if you are an agnostic or atheist.

Amazingly enough, the people who are agnostic or atheist usually, from my experience, are the ones most amazed and bewildered in a beautiful way when these mystical experiences happen to them.

Your journey to this Holy Land will not mirror mine. A host of different variables - your level of religiosity or spirituality; willingness to open yourself to new adventures; personal life experiences - will create your own unique experience.

One of my life missions was to visit the holy places of the world (or what I thought were places that had special or spiritual energy. As an example, many Americans think Sedona, Arizona is such a place). By the time I reached my 70s, I had accomplished this difficult task; I found "hot spots" in a variety of places, from the North Pole to Ayers Rock in Australia. On the other hand, my trip to the Galapagos was amazing and educational but I did not have any mystical or spiritual experiences.

> *"...Don't be dead or asleep or awake.*
> *Don't be anything.*
> *What you most,*
> *what you travel around wishing to find,*
> *lose yourself as lovers lose themselves, and you'll be that."*
> *~ Farid ud-Din Attar, Sufi Poet[1]*

But of all my adventures/journeys across every continent, one location was unique and truly special. All of my spiritual experiences there arose from the three major religions. So, what is this revered place of where I connected so deeply? It is the Holy Land of Israel, which I hold so precious to my soul.

I especially recommend that older teens/young adults visit Israel; for in the United States today, too many parents are materialistic, in addition to being either secular or not religious at all. Youth today have very little sense of the supernatural; in times past, many families had a member who was a part time mystic, perhaps knowledgeable in tarot cards and otherworldly stories. Israel with its sacred holy spaces can be a tool for spiritual personal development. In fact, many Jewish and Christian organizations have special travel programs to Israel for young adults.

From having traveled the world, I pass onto you a piece of advice: travel as a pilgrim, not a tourist. I define a "pilgrim" as a person who is a humble seeker and open to new experiences. And when a new experience does happen, they accept it, believe in it and treasure it.

Get out from behind your camera or cell phone. Utilize your senses; smell, touch and feel the place. The world is not a museum. Embrace it all and expect the unexpected. Perhaps you too will be blessed with mystical experiences. However, no one has the ability to create these experiences; they are truly authentic. One cannot make them happen; they either happen or they don't.

VACATIONING WITH GOD

NOTE TO READER:

This book contains additional information regarding the sites visited that explains their historical past and value to the visitor today. Some of this material is also related to my own personal experiences or adventures. This information will be displayed as a footnote directly after the experience, versus at the end of the chapter so that like-minded material is located in the same place.

This book consists of two parts. Part One encompasses Chapters 1-9 and reflect both my, and others' personal experiences while in the Holy Land. By their very nature, these experiences are ineffable, mystical and amazing interpersonal adventures. As a person with a PhD in Depth Psychology, I believe they belong to the world of Freud, where many of one's experiences lie in the conscious ego, but all remain in the unconscious.

In some instances, I have guessed why these special experiences occurred. These are my thoughts and feelings only, which may or may not be true. But I have added them for you to judge, to see if they add any value to you.

Part Two is on a different plane of reality. Yes, it is still about the holy land – and includes the Jewish, Christian and Muslim collectives that co-exist in Israel - but the viewpoint is that of the collective. Thus, I believe these experiences belong in psychologist/philosopher Carl Jung's world, which is coined the Collective Unconscious.

JACK LIN

ISRAEL

THE TEMPLE MOUNT

PART I

ADVENTURES

CHAPTER ONE
ARRIVAL TO THE HOLY LAND

*SOMETIMES WE MUST TRAVEL FAR
TO FIND OURSELVES*

This was my first trip to the Holy Land and I was excited! After landing at Ben Gurion Airport, we went to the King David hotel in Jerusalem to rest and adjust from jetlag. Never having been there before, my wife and I booked a tour to familiarize ourselves with the country.

Our two-week journey would begin in Jerusalem and then travel counter clockwise around northern and central Israel before returning to Jerusalem for a full 3 days.

Jerusalem reminds me of the older cities in Europe. The central core of Jerusalem is called The Old City, which is surrounded by a wall, and one must enter through one of the many gates. Outside of the wall, Jerusalem is a modern city that sits on a hill.

Our first visit was to the Western Wall (aka Wailing Wall), which was very crowded. I sat at a distance and took it all in. It felt good to see Jews praying at their Holy site in the Holy Land: finally, after thousands of years in exile, they were freely allowed to visit their Holy places. I chose not to approach the Wall due to the crowds.

While I did not have a special or unique experience, one of the tour members did. Seated next to each other on the tour bus, Aaron (not his real name) said to me *"I've got to tell you something. I am not a religious person. To me, religion meant war and people being killed. I firmly believe religion causes wars, and therefore I followed none of the Jewish customs and traditions. I eat pork and so forth, but my wife wanted to go on this journey very badly, so here we are."*

He continued, *"When we arrived at a viewpoint overlooking Jerusalem, our guide suggested that we might have a spiritual awakening. I didn't. When we got to the Wall, you may recall that we were on a balcony overlooking it. Something was happening to me. I cannot really describe it, but I felt an invisible energy. So I got out my T'filin (a religious garment for praying) that I hadn't used since my Bar Mitzvah. My mother asked me to take it to Israel with me. As I put it on, I started to cry. I haven't cried in years. As a reform Jew, I felt that religion was more of an obligation than a personal emotional experience. I have to tell you, whatever you call it - experiencing the Deity; love; loving those around me; or love of Israel - I felt his phenomenal presence come into me and all my brethren."*

As I listened to his testimonial, I thought so this is what it is for any Jew, religious or not, to come back to the Holy Land of their ancestors.

This can extend to non-Jews as well. A couple of years ago, a young American man who is Christian had occasion to live in Israel for a time period; he has a PhD from Harvard and was teaching at Tel Aviv University. From a historical and tourist point of view, he visited the Wall. Upon coming into close proximity to it, he was completely overcome by emotion, so much so that he started to sob and collapsed to his knees. He had no control over what was happening, as he lay prostrate at the wall, crying uncontrollably. Several Orthodox Jewish men and Rabbis came over to him and tried to comfort him by patting his back. To this day, he doesn't know from where this wellspring of feelings arose.

"A full life will be full of pain. But the only alternative is not to live fully or not to live at all."
- *M. Scott Peck*

ADVENTURE ONE - THE NATIVITY/CHRISTIAN FOR A DAY
TOUCHING CHRIST'S STAR

My first unusual experience was in Bethlehem, the birthplace of Jesus. Being knowledgeable in the study of religions and ancient history, I was aware the exact birthplace of Jesus is in question. People with opposing opinions each consider their viewpoint as the definitive authority. It was the mother of Emperor Constantine, the mystic, Helena[2] who determined the commonly accepted location.

The Church of the Nativity was built above a cave, that many people believe to be the birthplace of Christ. After the tour bus parked, we walked a few short blocks to the Church. The building was in very poor condition, the exact opposite of the Vatican in Rome. I asked the tour guide why it was not kept up. He answered, "Rome doesn't care about it. In fact, Israel financially helps the monks and priests who run it because it supports tourism."

VACATIONING WITH GOD

CHURCH of the NATIVITY

As a result of extensive travel, I was accustomed to the opulence of churches in Europe and the Americas, and was ill prepared for the condition of the Nativity Church. Our tour guide informed us that three separate church groups share control of the church; a small Greek Orthodox priest marched us down many steps and into the birthplace of Jesus, known as "The Grotto." As I looked at the priest and the other priests in the church, I noticed their heads were bowed, they were quiet and humble, completely opposite to the priests I saw at the Vatican.

The Grotto had a low ceiling and smelled musty and damp. On a small platform, 2 feet high by 2 feet wide and 20 feet in length - the actual length of the Grotto - was a five-pointed gold star. I knew from prior studies, that the original star had been stolen over 100 years ago. It was quiet in the Grotto and our tour group of 20 was the only visitors. Since our group was Jewish, they exhibited only mild interest and filed out quickly. I however, knelt next to the star, closed my eyes and shifted into my prayer/meditation state. I reached out and touched the star... and immediately withdrew my hand - the star was hot to the touch! I was overcome by an immense state of emotion.

My scientific brain searched for a logical explanation; a source of heat must be warming it. The star was indeed surrounded by several candles. Closing my eyes once more, I touched the stone next to star; it was very cool to the touch (approximately 56 degrees Fahrenheit) and a reasonable temperature for that underground location. This time with my eyes open, I again touched the star to find it still warm. I withdrew my body in awe. I asked myself, how many others, if any, had this experience?

I wondered if this was one of the places on earth where people experience unusual or mystical marvels, such as in Sedona, AZ? I was blown away. No wonder Constantine's mother Helena identified this spot as Jesus' birthplace.

Several days later at the hotel by the Sea of Galilee, I saw my two guides at the hotel bar. They were my chronological peers, also in their early 40's. The driver of the bus spoke broken English but the tour guide was very fluent, having visited the States on many occasions. They accepted my offer of a drink and we began to chat.

Finishing our drinks, the guide asked me, "Jack, what happened to you at the beginning of our tour?" Puzzled, I asked him what he meant. He replied, "Do you remember what happened when we visited the Grotto, what happened by the star?" Still confused, I asked him to elaborate. "Jack, you acted like the Holy Rollers from the south, the Southern Baptists when they touch the star." He added, "There are 2 kind of tours and I thought you had signed up for the wrong one, thinking you were on a Christian tour."

I assured him of my Judaism and said the Grotto at the Nativity must be a mystical and powerful place, with sacred energies that make it a supernatural spot. I added that many people of all faiths must be drawn to its powerful glow. I then realized that my experience was not unique at all, but thousands of Christian Americans had encountered this powerful, yet peaceful energy.

I had several subsequent experiences of this nature while visiting the Holy Land. Some happened during my first visit while others occurred during later trips. Some of Israel's blessed and holy grounds affected me while others did not. During the course of this book, I will describe my spiritual experiences to the best of my ability, though truly, these are indescribable. I will also re-tell (and have described) stories told to me by other individuals who also had strange experiences.

The Sea of Galilee

Each experience as it happened to me was overwhelming. I could not believe this was occurring. I was strong enough to not be fearful, but I trusted in God, that in the Holy Land, I could have special feelings that were not everyday occurrences.

"Be prepared at all times for the gifts of God and be ready always for the new ones. For God is a thousand times more ready to give than we are to receive."

- Meister Eckhart

TOUCHING THE PATRIARCH'S TOMB
ADVENTURE TWO - VISITING HEBRON

I highly anticipated our visit to the Tomb of the Patriarchs, in the city of Hebron, which is located approximately 19 miles south of Jerusalem and is the largest city in the West Bank, and the second largest in the Palestinian territories after Gaza.

It is believed by historians, as well as Jews and Muslims alike, that the burial sites of Abraham, Isaac and Jacob lie within its boundaries.[3] Since my name Jack is the English equivalent of Jacob or the Hebrew "Yaakov," I was quite excited about our visit. Hebron is located within PLO territory so 2 Israeli soldiers accompanied our group. The actual burial site is underneath a mosque; and since we weren't allowed to enter the mosque, we were lead in via a side door.

This visit to Hebron and the Tomb of the Patriarchs was important to me; I have studied The Bible for many years and I had always questioned if the stories of Abraham, Isaac and Jacob were true or were myths.

Our group, being mostly comprised of Jews, spent a great deal of time here - it is one of the holiest spots for the Jewish religion. I patiently waited my turn. There are three huge blocks of stone, approximately 6 feet high by 6 feet wide by 10 feet long. It is believed that the bones of the prophets are entombed below these stone pillars. I walked around the circumference of each and waited for the crowds to disperse. I approached Jacob's tomb and closed my eyes, making physical contact with the tomb by pressing my forehead against the side of the tomb. I went into deep prayer/and meditation, and waited. Nothing happened.

Hebron - Tomb of the Patriarchs

VACATIONING WITH GOD

Nothing! I confess I was upset, that my ego had been bruised. I had expected some sort of a divine manifestation. I did not get an answer at that time and I also felt a bit cheated.

However, allow me to share with you the adventure of another individual named Jacob visiting the Tomb of the Patriarchs, and his life changing adventure.

Brian Weiss is a psychiatrist who uses past life regression as a tool to assist individuals in psychotherapy. He was working with a patient who had a near death experience following a devastating car wreck in Holland. The man, named Jacob, was a successful South American businessman in his 30s and he recalled the accident scene as if he were a third party observer. In fact, he stated that he floated out of his body and thus, vividly recalls the horrific aftermath.

He became aware of a golden light in the distance and as he approached it he saw a monk wearing a brown robe. The monk told Jacob that it was not his time to pass over that he had to return to his body. Jacob felt the wisdom and power of the monk who also related several future events and Jacob's life, all of which later occurred. Jacob was whooshed back into his body now in a hospital bed, regained consciousness and for the first time, became aware of excruciating pain excruciating pain.

In 1980 while traveling in Israel, Jacob, who is Jewish visited the cave of the Patriarchs in Hebron which is a holy sign to both Jews and Muslims. After his experience in Holland, he had become more religious and had begun to pray more often. He saw the nearby mosque and sat down to pray with the Muslims there. After a while he rose to leave. An old Muslim man came up to him and said, "You are different from the others. They rarely sit down to pray with us." The old man pause for a moment, looking closely at Jake up before continuing, "You have met the monk. Do not forget what he has told you." Five years after the accident and 5000 miles distant, an old man knew about Jacob's encounter with the monk, an encounter that had happened while Jacob had been unconscious.

One of the reasons I had come to Israel to determine if the Old Testament was true history or merely legend. Here at this critical spot, I personally had no answer. This experience and many others led me to the belief that you cannot expect mystical experiences to happen upon demand.

NOTE

The people closest to me were the founders of our nation, the patriarchs Abraham, Isaac and Jacob. They wandered over the length and breadth of the land with a staff in their hand, a knotted stick fashioned from the branch of an oak, the strongest and stoutest of trees.

The patriarchs were independent beings who walked alone. They left the homes of their parents, parted from their brethren, and embarked on their lonesome path. They carried a weighty burden – a new faith, a new nation, a new land…

Some 40 years later, in doing the research for this book, I discovered that the three huge blocks of stone do not contain the bodies of the Patriarchs.

More interesting, was the fact that the person involved in the search/archeological work was none other than the Israeli hero, Moshe Dayan! Since there was a small hole leading to the underground tombs, he had a 12-year-old girl go down the hole to explore the Caves of Machpelah. She found that the deep tombs were situated below a non-penetrable floor. Dayan goes on to state, "If indeed this is the authentic site of the Caves of Machpelah, the cave lies somewhere below the floor of the structure. The representational tombs seen in the halls belong to a much later period. They were built above a large subterranean chamber containing sepulchral niches, to which entry is forbidden."

VACATIONING WITH GOD

TOUCHING RACHEL'S ENERGY
ADVENTURE THREE - VISITING RACHEL'S TOMB

When traveling back to Jerusalem, we stopped in Bethlehem and visited Rachel's tomb.6 I had forgotten Rachel, the second wife of Jacob, as she is not buried with the others in the Tomb of the Patriarchs. Jacob labored for 14 years before being allowed to marry her, and she bore him 2 sons, Joseph and Benjamin. Rachel is crucial, in that King David and Jesus come from her bloodline.

The tomb is in a small building outside the center of town. As I exited the bus, I noticed a couple of Israeli soldiers on the roof across the street protecting visitors. This initially surprised me, as the site is held sacred by all three religions, Judaism, Christianity and Islam; however, the town is located within Palestinian territory.

As we entered the building, we saw a young woman deep in prayer. It was obvious she was highly religious and likely a member of the Hasidism, a branch of Orthodox Judaism.

Our guides told us that local Jewish women who are having difficulties bearing children visit the site and pray for help. We waited patiently and she left a few minutes later.

Similar to the Tomb of the Patriarchs, the pillar was approximately 8 feet in height, 8 feet wide and 12 feet in length. Everyone milled about the tomb. After 5-10 minutes, the crowd dispersed and most went back to the bus. I went to the back to the bus. I went to the back to the tomb, placed my head against the cool rock and began to meditate.

Then it happened. I heard a strong clear masculine voice in my mind. The voice said, "Your ancestors, Abraham, Isaac and Jacob traveled through these valleys as described in the Old Testament."[4]

JACK LIN

Rachel's Tomb

VACATIONING WITH GOD

"I WAS IN AWE!"

In my entire life, although I have been blessed with several numinous experiences, I have never had a voice from my SELF, communicate with me.

The enormity of the statement overtook me. Sitting here at Rachel's tomb later, despite it being thousands of years later, time became meaningless and all of history disappeared. I was in the same spot as Jacob and his children. Starting with the story of Abraham, the Bible is, in a sense, the autobiography of the Jewish people and God. Israel still flourishes with the energy of my forefathers (and yours, if you are Christian or Muslim) who inhabited these hills and valleys. In contrast to the movie set where Charlton Heston became Moses, this actual soil is where David and Solomon were Kings; where the stories of Old and New Testaments become alive and full of energy.

In the past, I had wondered if the stories in the Bible were true, as the narratives of Noah and Abraham predate the written word. How were these stories remembered and how did they not change? I'm sure you recall the childhood game called "Telephone" - where a child whispered a statement to the child sitting next to him/her; and the statement whispering went around the circle until the last person, who said it out loud. And every time, the statement was totally changed from its beginning. Indeed, some scholars believe there are two (or more) authors of the Book of Genesis - one calls the Hebrew God, *Yod-Hey-Vav-Hey* and the other calls God, *Elohim*. Additionally, Chapters 1 and 2 of Genesis have different introductions regarding creation.

Starting with Abraham, I am now convinced of the veracity of the biblical stories due to the revelation/voice I heard at Rachel's tomb. Before Abraham's time, myths and stories from different tribes had been combined, and there were many discrepancies. For example, there are two different stories of the Creation in the Book of Genesis. So how did the tribe of Abraham keep their stories on point before there was writing?

I believe the following is the answer. Many years ago, I attended a Buddhist wedding in Los Angeles. The two different sects of Buddhism are separated by geography and time (approximately 1500 years); yet religious songs can be perfectly maintained passed down through the generations. The wedding was officiated by priests from both sects, and when it came time to sing the Sutras of the Buddha, both priests sang in perfect harmony.

I realized by using song and music, the early scribes were not writers - because the written word was not yet invented. They used songs to maintain the exact words their fathers had sung to them.

Like the Jews, the Buddhist thought some of their religious material was too holy to be written down; it is only recently that the Sutras of the Buddha have been put on paper. Additionally, Jews have a tradition that some of the mystical revelations from God to Moses were only passed down from father to son; prophet to prophet and were never to be written down for public consumption.

We are not following a mythology, but are remembering true events as passed down to us by our ancestors. Initially, this occurred via song, and later, through the written word.

NOTE:

"I WAS IN AWE!" What/who had communicated with me in Rachel's Tomb? I believe it was part of my Higher Self, which is the normally hidden part of myself. The Deity in me.

NOTE:

In this book, I state most (but not all) of the experiences people have had occurred when they are praying or meditating. In prayer, many people request or ask for some succor from not only the Deity but also Catholic Saints, Jesus, Luther, Muhammad or Rachel.

VACATIONING WITH GOD

This usually is ineffective; since we are the creator of our own world/universe, when we ask for something, it's an internal admission that we lack something. Thus, we unintentionally give energy to, and promulgate, that lacking. Instead, many believe the proper way to pray is thank God for your blessings and glorify God, in whichever form you sense the Deity. In that process, you may have a transcendental moment.

Having spent nine years studying with Buddhists learning meditation, I have my own specific method of going into meditation that I can share with you. I close my eyes almost entirely and calm myself down by taking three to five deep breaths in order to achieve diaphragm movement. After I am physically calmed, I then look to calm my mind. This can be quite a challenge amidst many interruptions: noises, smells and your own thoughts. The Buddhists describe our never-ending thoughts as monkeys jumping around, screeching, chattering and moving from tree to tree! Allow each of your thoughts to come and go – do not fight them. Eventually they will stop and you will be left with a dark, soft, peaceful place.

Continue to breathe slowly, and follow your breath in and out for anything to happen. Sometimes your reward will be a moment of peace in an otherwise chaotic life. Other times, you may receive a gift from the Deity such as an understanding or a revelation, and you are able to grasp something you could not ever comprehend before. This is the method I use during my spiritual journey. I became a pilgrim whether I was honoring Krishna, or a Hawaiian God or Mary since they are all manifestations of the Supreme Deity we Hebrews call Yod-Hey-Vav-Hey. Having described two deeply spiritual adventures, I must make the comment, that sitting here 40–50 years later, they are as clear in my mind today, as they were when they happened. I can close my eyes and I am in the moment, reliving the numinous/holy experiences. At my age, I have forgotten many events in my life, yet there are special emotional experiences I, like you, will always remember. There are a few examples that stand out in my mind. The first was when I threw up in the gutter due to anxiety on my first day attending Brooklyn Technical High School. A second example is when I had my first flight in a Piper Cub, (a small two-passenger aircraft), another, was my wedding. Interestingly enough, each spiritual adventure I experienced has had so much emotional impact on me, that they are permanently etched in my memory as well.

NOTE:

It should be remembered, however that all memories have the rashomon effect and therefore may be imperfect. Although they remain the same in your memory of them.

CHAPTER TWO
SPIRITUAL EXPERIENCES

*THE NON-RATIONAL PART OF LIFE -
THE NUMINOUS EXPERIENCE*

Before moving forward with more adventures, allow me to share my belief on what I mean by a spiritual or religious experience.

The Spiritual Experience

A spiritual experience is an encounter with something or someone other than you that is not based upon the material world, nor through the normal five senses, mind and intellect.

This experience is also without the use of alcohol/drugs. It is a life-altering event that causes a shift in reality, and can profoundly change how someone sees him/herself in relation to the universe. Yet, typically, the occurrence isn't rational or logical to our Western minds and we are disturbed by this discordance. What are we to do?

A German philosopher Rudolph Otto[5] may provide an answer. Otto describes the need to separate our ordinary reality from religious or spiritual reality. Typically, when one says they have "faith in God," they are attempting to turn this intangible feeling state into a rational emotional experience. But a direct connection with the Deity is an abstract feeling state; standing before the sacred is an impalpable experience.

Otto gave this non-rational and non-sensory feeling a name: Numinous (from the Latin word, Numen, meaning divine power). Since these occurrences are induced by the revelation of divine power, the Numinous experience is something "holy other" and basically different than anything in our normal reality. He believes we should not view religion nor our belief in God in the same way we perceive other matters of our everyday life.

Rather, we can view God and the notion of religion as non-rational, induced by the revelation of divine power, a "holy other," different from everything else in our normal reality. Accepting Otto's premise that religious experiences are different – but neither crazy nor senseless – means we can give up the wresting match between rational and non-rational events and simply call them true, real and non-rational. Along I sat content in the beautiful darkness with the energy of the ancients palpable.

These lines, philosopher/historian Mircea Eliade[6] states in *Patterns of Comparative Religion* (1958), "the Deity manifests itself when humans become aware of the sacred. We immediately recognize that we are now in a sacred and profane space and time, completely separate from our everyday life of secular experiences."

Now having reconciled with the illogical nature of spiritual/religious experiences (they are supposed to be irrational!), it will be of benefit to know how these occurrences are quantified or operationally defined. According to psychologist/philosopher William James[7], a spiritual experience is comprised of four elements:

1. **Transient** - the experience is temporary and the person soon return normal frame of mind.
2. **Ineffable** - it cannot adequately be described with words.
3. **Noetic** - The person has learned something valuable via being knowledge that is typically hidden from human understanding.
4. **Passive** - the experience occurs to the individual without conscious co While activities such as meditation might make a religious experience likely, it cannot be turned on/off by will.

In my personal experience, James' definition is right on target. James points out that the special quality of mystical experiences can be disturbing to some people as they offer a glimpse of previous unknown territory. At the same time, they do provide a map to offer an understanding to that terrain, and how it fits into one's life and/or the universe.

While William James never discusses any of his own mystical experiences, he nevertheless points out that in order to identify with a feeling or an experience, one must have prior familiarity with that particular emotional state. For example, only those who have experienced the feeling state of being in love can truly understand the emotion behind an opera singer's performance.

James also points out a difference between mystics and those who are religious in a traditional sense by quoting Evelyn Underhill[8] who said, "… The conventionally religious seek to know about God; mystics seek to know of God."[9] James additionally points out that they seek this knowledge in their present lifetime, not after they have died or in their afterlife.

During the course of this book, utilizing the experiences of others and myself in the Holy Land of Israel, I hope to explain to future Israel travelers that sacred and secular (e.g. ordinary, everyday) encounters are equally valid approaches to experience our world. These two modalities of being affect us in our history, in our sociology, and in our religions. Individuals who have yet to experience a supernatural event may find some of these adventures hard to believe. And that's okay. Those of you who have had deep experiences using drugs, or given birth or survived a terminal illness may resonate more readily to the upcoming seemingly irrational experiences.

The great American psychic and modern-day prophet/mystic Edgar Cayce[10] had many numinous experiences. Cayce stated that "All of us, that's right, ALL OF US, have the capacity to have numinous experiences if we trust ourselves, go within and find this connection between ego and soul". Cayce could say that the soul of a man is microcosmic representation of mankind as a whole, just as a drop of water from the sea is a microcosm of the ocean. Man can bring forth the creative forces and create his own world from within the greater world.

Cayce would say that since the Creator creates all souls, faithfully we are all in his image.

It is my hope, via the following adventures, those individuals who have never had a non-rational, spiritual experience may obtain possible openness in which to receive one such experience in the Holy Land of Israel. I fully expect people who have had spiritual experiences to surely have more in the Holy Land, but I predict they will be unable ahead of time to determine where and when these will occur. The deep unconscious is connected to the soul. The soul in turn is connected to the Deity, who is in charge of allowing such experiences to become real to our ego consciousness. The Deity is alive and well in the Holy Land.

CHAPTER THREE
RESTING PLACES

DEATH HERSELF IS DARK AND SWEET
BUT THE THOUGHT OF HER BRINGS UP
MONSTERS OF THE DEEP

ADVENTURE FOUR – TOMBS OF
ANCIENTS – NORTHERN ISRAEL

One of the great excavations/discoveries* of Israel is the Tombs of the Hebrew Ancients, which leaves me in contemplation to this day.

The use of coffins and in-ground burial was not in practice until post biblical times. Yet, bodies could not be left unburied; the fear permeated the Old Testament, which bestowed curses for this breach, such as in Deuteronomy (28:26), "Thy carcasses shall be food unto all fowls of the air, and onto the beasts of the earth." Thus, caves were typically utilized as burial tombs.*

Ancient Israelite burial practices are indicative of the desire to remain with one's family and community after death. "Bury me with my fathers." (Genesis 49:29), requests Jacob to Joseph. This desire to be buried at least in one's native land and preferably with one's ancestors was a constant refrain of the ancient Israelites. It is my understanding that the ancient Hebrew believed this practice was the way the soul would remain within the family of the Jewish collective.

Cave Exterior

Cave Interior

VACATIONING WITH GOD

During our tour, some in our group chose not to enter the tomb, but I found I was anxious to explore the deep, dark recesses. The entrance to the tomb is a medium sized cave that had been hollowed out by man as well as nature; it hasn't been used during recent times. We walked about 100 feet into the darkness and entered an area that had numerous flat rocks carved out of the mountain. The guide informed us that the Hebrews entombed their dead, including members of the Sanhedrin**, in these caves.

I asked to remain a few minutes more as our group started meandering towards the daylight. Our guide was kind enough to loan me a flashlight without which I would have been unable to see a thing.

Oddly enough, instead of finding the tomb cold and uninviting, a room reminiscent of gloom and death, I felt comforted, warm, safe and not at all fearful. My emotional brain wanted to reject this; after all, tombs are thought to be ghoulish and not a place one would expect to feel at home. I sat content in the beautiful darkness with the energy of the ancients palpable.

Reflecting back now, it is strange to me that Israel, located in a region with many days of sunshine had left me with so many spiritual adventures in dark places.

I realized the afterlife, and the transformation from this world to the beyond is nothing to fear. NOTHING TO FEAR AT ALL! This revelation, belonging in the grey area between philosophy and theology, was something to be pondered. In this dark place, I was certain that death shouldn't be viewed with trepidation. All the fear and anxiety was gone from my own ego/self. Our tour guide interrupted my reflections; it was time to move on.

JACK LIN

ADVENTURE FIVE - THE TOMB OF ABSALOM

Many years later on a different trip, while I was socializing with friends in the Kidron Valley outside Jerusalem, one of them suggested that we visit Absalom's tomb. Absalom was the rebellious son of King David, who earned the hatred of Jews, Muslims and Christians alike. It was a hot day, and if nothing else, the cool temperature of the tomb would be worth the visit.

The monument cast a shade upon the ground, and standing in its shelter, the sun became less powerful. Upon entering the tomb, we immediately felt its cooling relief. Barely inside by a few steps, I experienced a strange physical sensation: the hair on the back of my neck stood up. Growing up in a rough neighborhood of the Bronx, NY, I realized this as an indication of danger - my "fight or flight" response had been activated, and I immediately exited the tomb.[11]

My friends laughed as I spoke of my discomfort and feelings of uneasiness inside the tomb. It was only later than I learned that local passerby (Jews and Palestinians) would throw rocks at the tomb, and bring recalcitrant children there as a warning of what might happen to them if they did not behave.

For me, that particular tomb was a very negative place. Later that evening, I recalled my first visit to the Hebrew Tomb of the Ancients, and thought about the difference in energy between the tombs of the Ancients' and that of Absalom's. Despite going into the silent cave 100 feet in total darkness (we did have flashlights), The Tomb of the Ancients left me feeling warm and comforted.

I realize it is easier to have a spiritual experience in darker places than in the sunshine. We are so attached to living our lives mostly by the sense of sight. This relates to our ego and consciousness; thus, it is difficult for the deeper part of ourselves to break through. Non-logical experiences can happen in the daylight or sunshine, but generally these experiences are more likely to happen in the night or darkness.

VACATIONING WITH GOD

Absalom Tomb

VACATIONING WITH GOD

An Israeli's Woman's Point of View

On a different trip to Israel, a friend, an America-born Jew who at age of 30 made "aliyah" with his wife and children, escorted my partner and me. Sam (not his real name) took us to the borders of Lebanon and Syria, showing us the military fortifications and readiness. As a very aggressive Zionist, he then took us to areas that cause tremendous upset with the Palestinians, such as the settlements on the West Bank.

Unlike the Kibbutzim which are located in valleys, these settlements were situated on top of small hills/mountains. I asked why were they located in such a difficult place to build; he laughed and said, "and you are military?" I replied I was in the Air Force, not the Army! He explained these sites were strategically selected because of their defensive posture and prominence over the land. "Oh," I said, "A modern day Masada." "Yes," he replied, "and we will continue to control the West Bank."

I later talked with his wife – they lived in a small apartment in the Jewish section of Old City of Jerusalem. She told me that her husband continuously kept after her to make "aliaha" until she finally agreed. In order to live a normal life, they had to learn how to move beyond the anger of the Palestinian attacks.

I asked her a key question: did she feel closer to God living here? Her response was unexpected. "Yes, I feel we don't have to go to synagogue as we are living and eating of the land; we are in God's bosom." I then asked about the Israelis who leave and come to the US. She said, "If you are not very religious, the hardships of Israel are difficult to endure. While it is minor, she stated it took some time get used to the toilet paper! She then said, "Now I understand Sam's feelings. We stay here because we Jews belong to this land. The Deity brought us to this land and gave this land to us."

She continued, "After our release from Egypt, we accepted the 10 commandments, the blessings and the curse of God. We accept the Torah from our forefathers to our future generations, to which my children represent. This land is so different than America. You can look in the Bible, find a place and then visit it. You can go to Beersheba, or Bethel, and of course, in the middle of our city, the Western Wall and holy Mount Moriah/Temple Mount."

During this same trip, my partner, Sam and I visited the Mount of Olives. It is Jewish tradition to be buried there; it was prophesized that the Messiah (the second coming of Christ to Christians) will appear at this location and the Day of Judgment and the Resurrection of the Righteous will occur.

Since my mother had recently died, I brought an article of her clothing and my father's prayer shawl to bury on the hill. After finding an empty place, we realized the only digging tool was Sam's small penknife. A Palestinian gentleman several feet away spoke to us in Arabic and put up 2 fingers. Sam understood his words, which were to wait a few moments. He left and shortly returned with a shovel, and helped us dig an appropriate hole. Sam led us in a Jewish ritual and prayer and the Palestinian joined us. Afterward, I gave him a few shekels, and with Sam's help, thanked him in his language. Later that evening, I told my partner and Sam what an interesting day it had been; as a Jew on a previous trip, I had joined a Muslim ritual, and today a Muslim was part of our Jewish ritual. The world truly is a circle when you stand back and view it.

NOTE:

During my trips, I visited many sites which had been excavated such as Solomon's stables and Jericho. They were interesting from a scientific point of view, but left me with no puzzles to ponder.

It appears ancient Israelites placed great importance upon a decent burial. This presumed not only by the amount of references made to the fear of being unburied and curses for not abiding by this covenant in the Old Testament, but also by Abraham's purchase of the Cave of the Patriarchs, measures taken by later patriarchs to ensure they were buried there and that the biographies of Israelites typically ended with an account of their burial after stating their death had occurred.

The predominant tomb was a natural cave or chamber cut into a soft rock near the city. Rock shelves were chiseled into three sides of a chamber, and the bodies were laid face upward upon them, though others were laid on the floor. The same family used the tomb for generation upon generation; in order to make room for new burials, some skeletons were placed into a side chamber while others were discovered heaped up along the sides of the cave.

Neither the practices of cremation nor embalming were carried out by the ancient Israelites. Thus, despite no Biblical evidence regarding how soon burial took place after death, it is likely burial took place within a day after death due to the climate of the region.

Sanhedrin - The group of 23-71 appointed men in every city in the Land of Israel who served as courts of judges, given full authority over the people to carry out God's words and establish law. Our Supreme court is copied from the Sanhedrin; our founders were well groomed in the Old and New Testament.

CHAPTER FOUR
SPIRITUAL PLACES

WRESTLING WITH GOD

For millions of years, we were animals living on instinct; our conscious minds had yet to be developed. As we evolved, we became aware that certain locations were special and had power; as primitive people, we believed that Gods lived in these locations. There were the Gods of the valleys, Gods of the mountains and Gods of the rivers. The Hindus today believe that the Ganges River is a living God. All notable religions believe there are special places of worship that are deemed holy.[12] Primitive people were under the control of their unconscious mind, now called numinous experiences - just as we say animals are under the control of their instincts - as evidenced by writings of the ancient Hebrews, Greeks and Hindus. Man was able to talk to God; additionally, large animals that were very powerful were given Godlike qualities. As we moved from hunting/gathering to farming and herding, we began to possess a level of sophistication that grew with time.

In the last 4500 years, we recognize that the Great Spirit, the God of Creation and origin of man were one force, what 4 major world religions (Christianity; Judaism, Islam, Hinduism) called a monotheistic (one supreme God) God. Despite the many differences between them, the foundation of all four is the same: that God is one, and all things are born from that oneness. During this time of worsening religious extremism, if everyone focused on our basic commonality – that we all love, pray to and are loved by the same Deity – religious tolerance would develop.

There are many places throughout the world that are known to have mystical and spiritual energy.[13] Instinctively, we know that there are other forces/energies greater than those felt by our five senses.

Upon arrival to one of these locations, we intuitively know it is sacred, and feel a striking and inspiring power that invites contemplation of our souls. In its presence, we ask ourselves these questions: who are we, what are we doing here, from where have we come, where are we going, and what are we to accomplish in this life?

Literally, what are these sacred spaces? To me, they are locations with a literal and physical presence; be it something made by nature/ the Deity, or man. Examples of man-made objects are large statues, complex mosques, beautiful cathedrals, or unique buildings, (such as the Taj Mahal). They are physical embodiments of mans' genius trying to capture the Deity's feeling from his soul. Those who designed and built these monuments gained a miraculous insight on the deepest level, and sought to cast their feelings into stone, bronze and steel.

These sacred sites possess both peace and power. I have visited many of them and sometimes had non-logical experiences. However, by far, the most occurred in the Holy Land of Israel.

NOTE:

I have found that certain physical movements – such as the spinning by the Whirling Dervish[14] - can sometimes evoke a ritual, and move us into an energy field such as found at sacred spaces. I have been fortunate enough to experience (e.g. taste, touch and become hypnotized by) this process in deserts, in a sweat lodge, on the water, in a house of worship and in the Grand Canyon. When this transformation occurs, your ego completely loses control. Instead, the energy field regulates the action and you are led by the God-Head.)

VACATIONING WITH GOD

Man traces his roots to Africa. The first sapiens, born erect or not, and in Tanzania or Ethiopia are questions for anthropologists. This primitive man, as well as the later Homo sapiens, marched out of Africa via the land we call Israel today. It is the only place that connects Africa and Asia, eventually leading to Europe. In essence, Israel was the pathway to the world.

Despite its tiny size,[15] its history mightily graces the annals of mankind and its religious significance cannot be understated, towering above enormous countries many times its size. Why? Because man met the Deity on its desert soil. This divine - human encounter created holiness; "holy," meaning where

God is available to man.

The "Old City" of Jerusalem, the Golden City, that "City on the Hill" is probably the most fought over piece of real estate in the world. Less than 1 square mile, it is to this day, divided into four unequal quarters governed by Jews, Christians, Muslims and Armenians. It was under the reign of King David – descended from the Tribe of Judea and ancestor to Jesus - that the city became a designated Holy site. As we know from the Old Testament, David had a special relationship with the Deity. His decisive win in the battle with Goliath indicated to the Hebrews that the Deity was on his shoulder.

However, 1000 years earlier, God had commanded Abraham to sacrifice his son Isaac on Mount Moriah, the location of the Foundation Stone.[16] Later this location became the site of the First Temple also known as Solomon's (son of King David) Temple.

The territory of Israel has been of the utmost importance over many millennia; it has been attacked, conquered and occupied by numerous factions since ancient times. From the Syrians, the Mesopotamians, the Byzantine Empire, the Greeks, the Romans and the Ottoman Empire to the Crusaders. It was only recently returned to the Jews after the British Mandate of Palestine ended in 1948; immediately thereafter, a war over territory ensued between a coalition of Arab armies and the Jews, who had established the land as the State of Israel after the British withdrew.

Due to the whole of its history, and especially being the birthplace of the world's major religions, pilgrims from many different religions flock to Israel

– to pray, pay homage and visit the sites so hallowed within their beliefs. And while visiting and meditating upon these sacred places, religious/spiritual experiences can be had by those who seek them.

If you are looking for an experience that will reveal, "What's it all about, Alfie," visit Israel. Life itself is a miraculous experience. If you have been present at the birth of a child, then you will have a sense of this numinous energy. Life is not a meandering path through the countryside without direction. It is designed by our soul to teach us love, and to overcome fear and unfortunately, for many the resulting reaction is the need to have power. Life is an existential and personal battle; and to this day, Jerusalem and Israel continue to be site of this ongoing struggle. Due to Israel's numinous power, pilgrims will have the greatest opportunity to understand this wrestle with

God.

"Enchantment is a spell that comes over us, an aura of fantasy and emotion that can settle on the heart and either disturb it or send it into rapture and revelry"
- Thomas Moore

Mr. Moore, who was a monk in a Catholic Religious Order, believes that the soul needs regular excursions into enchantment. I agree… On the top of a ski mountain; in the middle of a large ocean, I feel I am feeding my soul.

The fact that you are reading this far into this book means you are following a magical journey to open the door to yourself.

CHAPTER FIVE
WALLS AND WELLS

DRINKING HOLY WATER

ADVENTURE SIX - MARY'S WELL IN NAZARETH

The following adventure transpired over the course of two years. While it's an old and a typical desert town from western perspective, Nazareth was one of the most interesting places on our tour. The city features a working well, something rarely seen in an America town today. Local women come to draw water for their families as they have for thousands of years. This well is called Mary's Well after the Virgin Mary; it is reputed to be the location where the angel Gabriel appeared and told Mary that she would bear the Son of God.

We were offered a drink from the well; most of the Jewish tourists declined but I gratefully accepted the cool refreshment, as it was a blistering hot day. It tasted wonderful and I savored the moisture it offered. I took another drink and waited for some sign, however small, since this water came from the blessed place. Nothing happened. *Oh well*, I thought, pun intended, a typical tourist trap. Maybe I wasn't holy enough, or perhaps spiritual experiences at this site were reserved for those of the Christian faith.

Upon entering the bus, I was gripped with an overwhelming urge to draw the well. I picked up a tourist brochure and began to sketch it. In the past, my artistic muse had emanated most frequently through poetry, and I have published a poetry book. Yet overall, my artistic talent ranked quite low on my list of skills. Much to my astonishment, the rudimentary drawing was quite good.

I returned to the States and took several courses in oil painting hoping to refine my technique. I reflected upon the fact that I hadn't written a poem in over a year. Could Mary's well have been responsible, as I now felt the urge, and indeed a necessity, to express myself on canvass. I was now deep into a psychological process, wrestling with my own psyche and was unsure what the end product would look like.

Two faces of the Deity emerged: a loving face and a hateful face; a light face and a dark face; a beautiful face and a terrible face. I wasn't sure what to do with the painting. A deeply religious friend asked if he could have it and I was happy to give it away. I still do not understand the meaning of Mary's Well and drinking of its waters. I only know that it affected me profoundly and continues to affect me to this day.[17]

Now, in reflection as an older, wiser, and more experienced person, I believe I was given the deep understanding that we live in a duality. In order to understand our universe and reality, we must have the ability

VACATIONING WITH GOD

to acknowledge dualities such as high/low; cold/hot; light/dark. With an ability to sense and appreciate opposites, we can, with wisdom, understand the difference between states. Everything is indeed on a continuum, but with our limited point of view, we tend to only see one direction or the other. (On a personal note, with this painting, my days as a canvas painter ended. Today, when I have an emotion, which needs to be expressed, it is in poetry, papers, and now in this book.)

When we can simultaneously see both sides of the duality, we can extricate from our ego selves, move to our higher self and understand the universe of God is complete and perfect. Therefore, we understand the Dao (Tao) - light begins within the dark, and dark begins within the light.

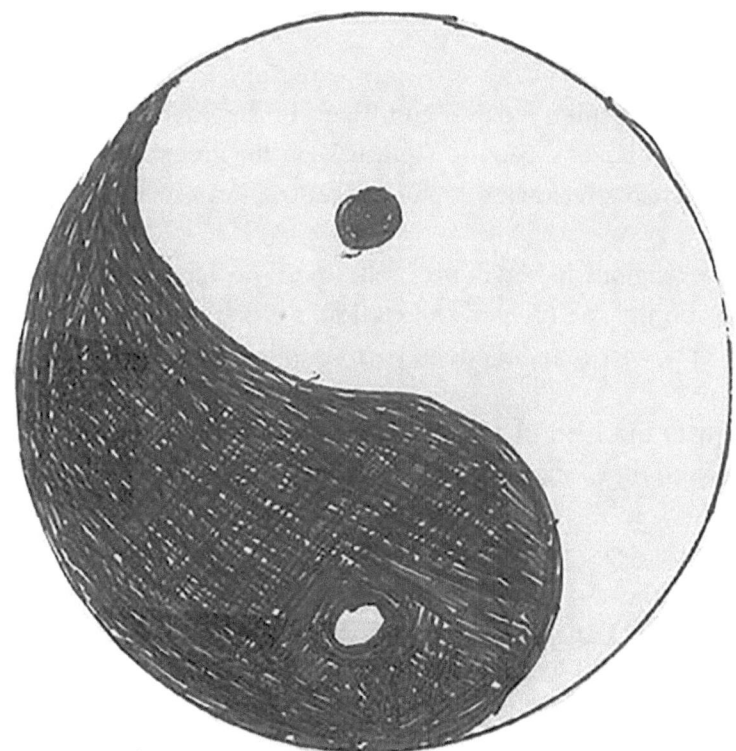

Duality as expressed by Lao Tse

TOUCHING HOLY STONE
ADVENTURE SEVEN – THE WESTERN WALL

After making a loop through the county, our tour returned to Jerusalem. Since I hadn't spent much time at the Wall upon our arrival to Israel, I very much looked forward to spending some serious time there and on the Temple Mount.

In Judaism, the holiest place on earth is the Western Wall, which has become a dedicated place of pilgrimage for the Jews. It is all that remains of Second Temple*, destroyed by Romans after the siege in 70 CE. After this building of great splendor was leveled, only a 25-foot outer perimeter high wall remained. In essence, the Western Wall is a retaining wall of the Temple Mount.

The Temple Mount is a very holy center of faith to the three major religions: Christianity, Judaism and Islam. In the Bible, it is also known as Mount Moriah and Mount Zion. It is on the grounds of the Temple Mount where many powerful religious experiences occurred.**

Many religious Jews will not walk upon the Temple Mount; as the prior location of the Holy of the Holies, it is believed that some aspect of divine presence remains and as such, is to be avoided.

My wife and I left our hotel located outside the Old City walls and took a cab to the Dung Gate. We approached the Wall, and as required, separated – I, to the Men's' side and she, to the Women's' side. I looked around at the Jews, praying in different styles. Some were young, some old, some with stern faces, others smiling and some were crying. No Bar Mitzvahs were taking place so it was much quieter than the last time I visited.

I then approached the wall to pray. As it is my practice, I began my method of prayer/meditation; I closed my eyes, took several deep breaths and placed my forehead against the wall. As I touched my head, a voice screamed out in Hebrew; since I didn't understand, I kept praying. An arm grabbed my shoulder and a young bearded man dressed in the traditional black Hassidic attire stated in English I was not allowed to pray that way. He said one is allowed to stand by the wall - or may sit due to age - and may touch it and place small written prayers into its crevices (hoping the Deity will see/hear these prayers). However, one cannot place one's forehead against it.

I responded, that I was an American and this was how I prayed, but he said it was unacceptable. Being the foreigner, I backed off. I took a few steps back and said to the Deity, "I came a long way to pray here." Then, nature, the Deity, and/or good fortune happened: it started to rain! It didn't bother me as it was a warm rain, but everyone else began to back away to get under cover. I saw my wife and other women move to a back wall underneath a balcony. As the rain became a downpour, I noticed everyone left, including the Guardians of the Wall. As I walked back to the Wall, I laughed to myself and thanked the Deity. I now had the wall to myself and put my forehead against. It was becoming wet yet still warm from the sun.

In my mind, I immediately saw dark caverns full of ancient Israeli artifacts such as rituals objects and ornaments. Logically, I knew buried below the wall were items from the ancient Hebrew temples. While I received no other information, I knew the Wall had power.

Unlike so many others, I did not cry at the Wall, and I wondered why not. Weeks later, I recalled that in the early afternoon, we had visited Yad Vashem, Israel's official memorial to victims of the Holocaust. While at the museum, I cried during the entire visit, and never in my life had I cried this way. The memorial describes the people, the events, and the annihilation of 6 million innocent lives. Even as a child, I never cried for 2 – 3 hours straight, but I do not consider it a spiritual experience. It was deeply emotional. All the visitors I saw that day cried as well.

JACK LIN

The Western Wall

It was beyond my ability to comprehend their suffering and death as they were destroyed not by nature's chance, but by the complete brutality of other human beings - humans who, up to that point, were civilized, possessing the latest Western technology. That evening when I was the Wall, I understood the Wall's glory and defeat, the light and the dark it represents, and the beauty and ugliness of the Judeo-Christian foundation. The Wall has great power from two sources: 1) the masses who visit and pour their love and sorrow for the millions who had died, and 2) from the ancients that had created it from the glory days of Jerusalem.

Many years later, I revisited the Wall and witnessed this power, which I will describe in *ADVENTURE EIGHT.* Additionally, also years later, I read that during excavations, Israeli archeologists had found Temple remnants below the wall. So my vision was fairly on target.

As I reflect back, I realize my experiences were both Jewish and Christian… would I ever have an Islamic one?

The first temple, called Solomon's Temple, was destroyed in 586 BCE during the Babylonian invasion.

The Foundation Stone and its implications; where Abraham fulfilled his duty to God by offering up his son Isaac for sacrifice; where the Prophet Mohammed embarked upon his inspiring Night Journey/assent to heaven with the Angel Gabriel. In addition, inside Solomon's Temple, a sacred area called the Holy of the Holies contained the stone tablets upon which God had etched the 10 Commandments and gave to Moses.

JACK LIN

Vad Vashem

CHAPTER SIX
THE TRIP TO MOUNT SINAI

TOUCHING GOD'S MOUNTAIN

I was on a very special trip of the Holy Land in 1992 with 17 other congregants of my small Renewal Synagogue in Los Angeles, led by our spiritual Rabbi. The Rabbi picked our roommates; mine was a young Jewish doctor, born in Egypt, who had migrated with his family to the United States 20 years earlier. The tour was to simulate and understand the trek taken by the Hebrews from Egypt to the Land of Milk and Honey.

At first, we landed in Cairo and spent several days exploring its numerous tourist attractions, including the Great Sphinx, the old Ben Ezra Synagogue, the Step Pyramid and the Great Pyramid of Giza.

Next on the itinerary was Mount Sinai, located in the southern portion of the Sinai Peninsula. Americans who have visited our great deserts would have difficulty imagining the Sinai. US deserts typically contain some cactus, yucca and perhaps some Joshua trees, and an enormous amount of sand. In contrast, the portion of the Sinai we had visited was all rock. Above the plain were big rock mountains, and the plain below was filled with smaller sized rocks, dwindling all the way down to pebbles.

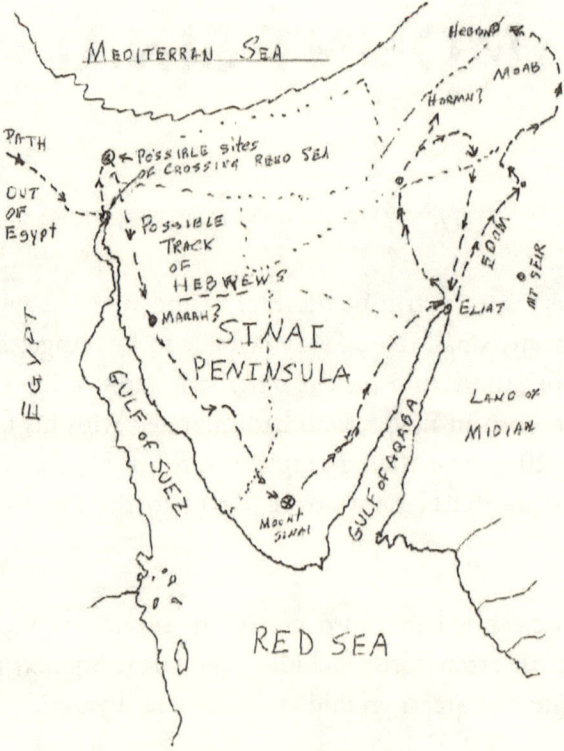

Drawn by Author

VACATIONING WITH GOD

The Sinai is part of Asia, bordered on the west by the Suez Canal, and on the south and the east, by the Red Sea. It is a dry, barren land devoid of inhabitants; on rare occasion, one might encounter a Bedouin.

The Sinai became sanctified after Moses freed the Hebrew slaves from Egyptian rule and led the Israelites into its desert land. They resided here for 40 years and as God's chosen people, were to abide by the laws famously engraved upon the stone tablets given to Moses. Those rules, which covered all aspects of daily life, became known as the Ten Commandments.

We were brought into the southern portion of the Sinai desert via several station wagons driven by Egyptians with two Israeli men leading this leg of the trip. When Israel occupied the Sinai Peninsula from 1967 – 1982, they had been assigned to the Israeli National Park Service and had been stationed here in the Sinai.

We were to spend almost a week camping; there were no accommodations in the region. Having camped many times, I quickly organized my personal belongings, wandered away from my group and climbed up a small hill. After reaching the top, I looked over at a broad vista of nothing. There were mountains, rocks and sand as far as the eye can see. I walked down the other side of the hill and was then completely isolated from our campsite.

Much of Israel is desert, which is a very strange place. The Sinai and the desert below Bethlehem appear as if they are devoid of all vegetation and life. The silence is deafening, and you feel miniscule in comparison to the vast, flat land. Our normal frame of reference with ego information, personal unconscious information and our collective information is missing. Despite reaching several summits of high mountains in the US and Europe, going above 15,000ft in the small hills of Katmandu, Nepal and traveling to the all the great oceans in addition to the North Pole, I never felt so trivial and inadequate until I met the Sinai. The desert was just too big for me at that point in my spiritual development.

An explanation of finding God in the desert was written 100 years ago by Lawrence of Arabia.* Lawrence described a similar physical sensation of a presence in his autobiographical account, *The Seven Pillars of Wisdom* while in the deserts of the Middle East during military service.

In order to enhance understanding of the desert experience, I will share a story by another desert journeyer, Joan, (the friend of an acquaintance of mine). Joan had a vision of a man in the desert, and felt compelled to find him. (As an aside, I have met many individuals who received a calling from/had a vision of a particular Hindu Yogi, and others who traveled to India and met their Master who had appeared to them in a vision.)

Upon arrival at the desert, Joan went over a small hill and felt something unique; a pulsation of sorts through her body that she felt was the essence of God. I recalled that Lawrence described a similar physical sensation of a presence.

As reported by my acquaintance, Joan told her that she had a dream while camping out in the desert the night of her arrival. In the dream, Jesus came to her. He informed that she had all the tools she needed to work out her life. From my own spiritual endeavors, I know it is not uncommon for people to dream of Jesus. Typically, he appears to impart a message that helps them to resolve a problem that they were struggling with. From my studies in Depth Psychology, I interpret Jesus to be an archetype of a sage.

In her dream, Jesus gave Joan two stones, and at first, she didn't understand why. Then, Jesus told her telepathically, without words, that the stones represented materials of the world.

Joan awoke in the morning, and was unclear of the meaning of her dream. As she walked to her car, something on the ground caught her eye. Right next to the driver's side door were 2 stones, exactly like the stones she had seen in the dream! She bent down, picked them up and realized she was living through a miracle; the two stones fit together perfectly, and had been a single stone that had split apart.

VACATIONING WITH GOD

She immediately had a revelation: that when we are created, we possess both a material and a spiritual life that appear different to us, but are in fact the same.

My interpretation of her experience is the following: that in the midst of our seemingly all-encompassing everyday life of the material world, we must make an effort to support our spiritual lives. We need to remember we are messengers of the Deity. As such, we ought to be generous in our love for others; for each face we see is another face of God.

We had our first dinner in the Sinai; poignantly, the Rabbi brought matzah to share and I brought a canteen of kosher wine so we celebrated our ancestors and ourselves in this place so desolate, yet so full with collective memories.

The next day, our small caravan of three station wagons, traveled to a large oasis, within which several Bedouins families lived. They graciously allowed us access to their water; our Israeli guides had brought them bags of flour, sugar and salt for the privilege of both visiting with them and camping in their environment. As a treat, the Bedouins made us bread using the tops of 55 gallon drums…and it was the most delicious bread I have ever eaten! Was it due to being in Sinai, or the sharing with a primitive, passionate people?

Two days later, we visited Saint Katherine's monastery at the base of Mount Sinai. Commissioned by Emperor Justinian, it is over 1500 years old and considered to be the oldest functioning Christian monastery in the world. Currently, it is in the care of Greek Orthodox monks who claim to posses Moses' original burning bush. At one time, it housed the *Codex Sinaiticus*, a fourth century version of the *Septuagint*. Although situated in Arab territory, it has never been attacked; both Muslims and Christians hold in high regard and deem it to lie on Holy ground.

We camped there over night. I recall that in the morning, there was a brief window of time during the sunrise when the light hits the trees and bushes at just the right angle. For a brief moment, they are outlined in a

Mount Sinai

VACATIONING WITH GOD

silver light, which makes them appear as if they were on fire. I wondered if that phenomenon caused Moses' bush to appear as if on fire. But then I remembered that the bush burned throughout his entire conversation with the Deity, not just an instant.

ADVENTURE EIGHT (A) – CLIMBING MOUNT SINAI

In the morning, we prepared to ascend the Sinai, which rises 7500 feet from the desert floor. Built by the Saint Catherine's monks, 2700 rocky steps lead to the summit. We were intent on performing a mystical experience: to carry a Torah up to the peak of Mount Sinai. Being of an older generation, we took a less heavy, smaller Torah. Although by far the oldest, I was in the best physical shape of my senior life. The first part of the journey was not difficult we rode on the back of camels. But halfway up the mountain, the camels could go no further; we had many hundreds of step to go on foot. Half of the group were already exhausted from the physically demanding journey and had decided to opt out of the ascent; they would instead wait for us.

The temperature at Mount Sinai that day was a fairly constant 80°. As the mountain faces north, there was no direct sunlight on us. We were halfway up when catastrophe struck. My stomach was bubbling and churning - it was Montezuma's revenge! Everyone had been ill with the stomach flu at some point during the trip, myself being the one exception. Now it was my turn and it could not have hit at a worse time. There were no restrooms on the path; this could prove to be quite embarrassing. I told the Rabbi to proceed without me, that I would linger behind and catch up later. I allowed them to put several hundred feet between us and then I relieved myself behind a scraggly bush. Twice more I found it necessary to decorate the Holy mountain in a most "Unholy fashion". Weak and exhausted, I kept trudging up the stairs.

As I climbed alone, I started to see human faces[18] in the rock, clear and defined, approximately 6' x 6'. In the rock forever, I thought, in a strange sort of purgatory. The faces were seeing and feeling the sunrise, day in and day out on Moses' mountain.

VACATIONING WITH GOD

I continued to climb and finally reached the summit; it was not what I expected. First, there was a locked, rock building, the monks' Chapel. It was said to contain the rock from which the stone tablets of the 10 Commandments were hewn. Second, it was a mess: trash and debris of every category littered the area. Definitely, culture shock to us American tourists and pilgrims. We cleaned up the area as best we could. Then we commenced our ritual - from our little Torah, we read the 10 Commandments, given from the Deity to Moses on the top of this mountain, upon which we stood.

I went into a dream-like state; I looked up at the clouds and thought I could see angels. I assumed I was hallucinating from the climb. Then I heard something in my mind, which I had forgotten, but now it came in loud and clear in my head. It was the 23rd Psalm.

The LORD is my shepherd I shall not want.
He maketh me lie down in green pastures; He leadeth me beside still waters.
He restoreth my soul; He guideth me in straight paths for His name's sake.
Yea, though I walk through the valley of the shadow of death,
I will fear no evil for Thou art with me;
Thy rod and Thy staff, they comfort me.
Thou preparest a table before me in the presence of mine enemies; Thou hast anointed my head with oil; my cup runneth over.
Surely goodness and mercy shall follow me all the days of my life; and I will dwell in the house of the Lord forever

Why had I forgotten the verse, and why was I remembering it now?

The clouds around the mountain grew very dark and the heavens opened up. Amidst lightning bolts and thunderclaps, the rain poured down. My roommate Mark, said he wanted to remain at the top. So I left him there and began the dissent with everyone else. I must admit it was fun - I felt as though I was flying down the mountain. When we reached the bottom, I noted the weather was calm and clear on the plains, though still tumultuous at the summit. To primitive people, it must have looked like the Deity was at the top of the mountain.

I went to my sleeping bag, lied down and began to meditate. I was contemplating my human deposits left on the holy mountain. Lying on my back, I realized that no matter the amount of future rain, nor beating of the sun, nor time passed, that part of me - my DNA - will forever remain on the holy mountain. Anytime I desire, I can close my eyes and go back to the mountain. It is my experience and I can determine how much I wish to visit the mountain. I then feel as I am once again on the mountain, and am a part of the mountain. I can love the world and all of its contents.

ADVENTURE EIGHT (B) – THE CALL TO PRAYER (THE ADHAN) MUSLIM FOR A DAY

Another tourist group of 20-30 men from Cairo were also at Saint Catherine's Monastery. I heard them start the call to prayer. During my past world travels, I had been allowed to pray in the various churches, temples or synagogues I visited. But whenever I had asked permission to pray in mosques, I was told only Muslims could do so.

I called out to my Egyptian drivers, with whom by this time I was quite friendly, and asked if I could pray with the group. They said yes. I grabbed my beach towel to use as a prayer shawl and ran out to the group. The men were lined up in a platoon-like fashion out in the open, on the ground. One person in front of the group led the call to prayer. Since I didn't speak Arabic, I called out in English, "May I pray with you?" - and a voice in the group responded "Yes."

I laid my beach towel on the ground and started to mimic the men's actions. As the Muezzin continued his song, I felt a strange sensation; the entire left side of my chest started to tingle. Only once before in my life had I felt similar small pulsations within my chest wall - when I was sleeping with an open window to the Giza pyramid, in full moonlight. The feeling was not painful, nor was it similar to heart attack symptoms or a gastrointestinal issue. I was very conscious of these flutters. I said to myself, if they get painful, I would leave the prayer area. They did not and I remained on my beach towel.

The beauty of the call to prayer entered me. It was truly a magnificent piece of music sung by the leader, exquisite beyond words. My scientific brain wondered if the melody's splendor was due to it echoing off God's Holy Mountain behind me. If you have yet to hear it, go to YouTube and search for "Muslim Call to Prayer Music." Choose one, close your eyes and allow it to flow into you and around you. Allahu Akbar, Allahu Akbar - God is Great, God is the Greatest.

Later while doing research, I learned that Arabic is a vibrational language that depends on sound. Therefore, there is musicality to the words that is soothing, peaceful and almost hypnotic.

NOTE:

When you study Holograms and Particle Physics, as I have in my professional career, you realize matter at its core, is vibrational energy. Thereby, there are some sound energies/vibrations that can affect light forms. An example of this, if you sit in a room with several hundred people singing, "Hari Krishna-Hari Krishna", then you would understand this concept.

Now as I write this, I recall that President Barack Obama stated the most beautiful music he had ever heard was the call to prayer at sunset. The praying started and I felt very comfortable and accepted by my Muslim group. It should be noted that sunrise and sunset have holy energies to them. However, we "advanced" Westerners understand scientifically that the earth fully rotates every 24 hours so we have lost the ability to view sunrise/sunset as the miracle it is. We simply see the sunrise as the moment the planet turns eastward in which to receive light from the sun.

In contrast, primitive people recognized sunrise and sunset with special rituals; they believed the intersection of earth mother and the sun father occurred at that point/place in time. Those who meditates at dawn or sunset knows this enlightened period is perfect for analyzing your prior night's dream or the events of your day just passed.

Later that evening, another interesting event occurred. There was only one bathroom available to tourists in at the Monastery and our women wanted to use it to shower and dress. For some reason, the Rabbi asked me to be the guardian at the bathroom door while the women were inside. I wondered why he had not asked my Arabic speaking roommate; perhaps he wasn't around. In any case, a few minutes after the women entered, several men from the Egyptian Muslim group came to enter. I said no; women were inside. But since they didn't understand English, I mimed women's breasts and gestured that they were in there. Somehow, the men understood, and I turned away several more. I believe the fact I had prayed with them gave me the opportunity to be a successful guardian.

That night as I laid in my sleeping bag, I reflected back on the events of the day and started to meditate. I remembered experiencing the vibrations at the Giza Pyramid, and the sensation at the call to Prayer was similar. These were minute pulsations in the left side of my chest, thus, relating to my heart. I grappled with the notion that the Muslim religion is somehow anchored to the ancient Egyptians, although it began in the Arabian Desert (known today as Saudi Arabia). Islam is a physically and spiritually powerful force, and I now understand why these people – Arabs, Bedouins and Egyptians – are so passionate.

Their religion is alive to them, similar to the Hindus of India who still live within their Gods and not outside of them.

Due to recent oil wealth in the parts of the Middle East, perhaps a portion of the population will change their personal relationship to Islam. But it is likely the majority will still live in an impassioned state. For one day and one night, I was allowed to pick up the veil and enter this state of being. It is most beautiful and deadly. I realized why the Imams keep so strongly to their faith and the words of Muhammad; they recognize (consciously or unconsciously) that if they enter the West, a part of Islam and their relationship to their God, will be destroyed. From their perspective, they are in a fight for survival. And the United States is the great devil, and the small devil is, of course, our democratic partner of that region, Israel. I slept peacefully that night.

VACATIONING WITH GOD

NOTE:

Upon reflection, I realized that Western Civilizations are basically comprised of Christians, Jews and Muslims, who are all descendants of Abraham: Muslims via Abraham's first son Ishmael, Christians from the bloodline of King David and of course the Jews from Abraham's son and grandson, Isaac and Jacob. Thus, we all believe in one God.

The Islamic wars (Jihads) started in approximately 620CE; Islam burst out of the Arabian Peninsula into the (Christian) Middle East. Over the next few centuries, they continued to attack the classical civilizations of Rome and Greece. They conquered most of the Mediterranean and began to establish themselves throughout all of the Iberian Peninsula via Northern Africa. The Crusades (1095-1291CE) were an attempt by the Church to wrestle back the Middle East from Islamic rule.

By 1400CE, Islam had conquered a major portion of southern France. After the fall of Constantinople in 1453CE, Islam turned its attention back to Eastern Europe during the 1500-1600s, conquering territory within 100 miles of Vienna. In Switzerland and Spain today, one can see churches that look like mosques because they once were the houses of Muslin worship. Unfortunately, a small part of the religion - Islamic extremism - is actively at war with Western Civilization, due to vast cultural differences between (fundamentalist/extremist) Islamic Civilization and the Western world. This rift is now at a boiling point due to globalization; interactions between Islam and the West have increased at an alarming rate.

Western Civilization represents, and is the basis of, the advancement of mankind. In the 18th Century, an intellectual movement (the "Age of Enlightenment") began to dominate Europe. The campaign became closely associated with the scientific revolution; the source of authority became reason, which undermined the supremacy and power of the monarchy and the Church. Out of this Age came many ideals that we take for granted today such as freedom, the separation of church and state, constitutional government and tolerance for others.

In the United States, our forefathers purposely instituted mechanisms in our governing documents to allow for societal shifts. For example, we have the capacity to amend our Constitution, and have done so many times over the past 240 years. Our society eventually adapts to change, thought it can be a painful and long process to treat all humans as equal regardless of race, creed, color, religion, gender or sexual orientation. Prime examples include women gaining the right to vote, interracial marriage, gay marriage and the right to have an abortion.

On the other hand, Islamic Civilization did not incorporate constitutional governments nor any of the other ideals associated with the Age of Enlightenment. Muslims rely upon Sharia Law (derived from the Quran and the Hadith) which was relevant when written 1500 years ago; however, it has no built-in methodology for change. The differences between these two systems - laws based upon a constitutional government versus Sharia Law - are immense and obvious to everyone.

However, historians might argue that the true conflict is an internal struggle within Islam itself, and not with Western Civilization. Might Islam modify itself and become more tolerant to others who hold different beliefs? The Imams who struggle with this possibility, rightfully fear change, for the elimination of fixed Islamic laws may destroy their religion.

After visiting Mt Sinai, we toured the southern portion of the Sinai and stopped at the Red Sea, specifically, the Gulf of Aqaba, approximately 60 miles south of Eilat. Since we again found the beach strewn with garbage, we fanned out and cleaned up the entire area. We then set up our campground, ate lunch and were given free time.

I went to the shore of the Red Sea and dove in, without mask, snorkel, nor fins. The water was warm and crystal clear and dense with fish of many different colors! Another unique aspect of this location was the beautiful sea floor; the deepest I had ever swam above. From just after the shoreline, the bottom plummeted into infinity. Lacking scuba equipment, I could only go down to approx. 10-15 feet. I felt as if I was on a vacation instead of a historical odyssey.

VACATIONING WITH GOD

The next day we crossed the border from Egypt to Israel, and I warmly thanked our Egyptian drivers. At the border crossing, there is a "no man's land" of about 30-40 yards - Israeli troops on one side and Egyptian troops on the other. I worked alongside our two Israeli tour guides and moved the group's luggage from one border to the other.

After finishing the task, I joined the group at lunch…but much of it had already been devoured (perhaps because it was far superior to the food in Egypt). No one thought to leave me any, the person who was hauling their luggage! It amazed me that people can be spiritual and thoughtless simultaneously. Even the Rabbi forgot about me. We had just been through this phenomenally uplifting experience in the Sinai, and now, having returned to Holy Israeli soil, reverted back to our customary behavior. I pondered why I had helped: was it to be helpful and caring, or was my ego involved to exhibit my physical prowess?

Throughout our camping experience, I felt superior to the others due to my numerous river-rafting/camping trips. Upon reflection, I paid a price for my hubris. Today, two artificial hips and one artificial knee (thanks to American football), would make it almost impossible for me to carry that luggage across that no man's land.

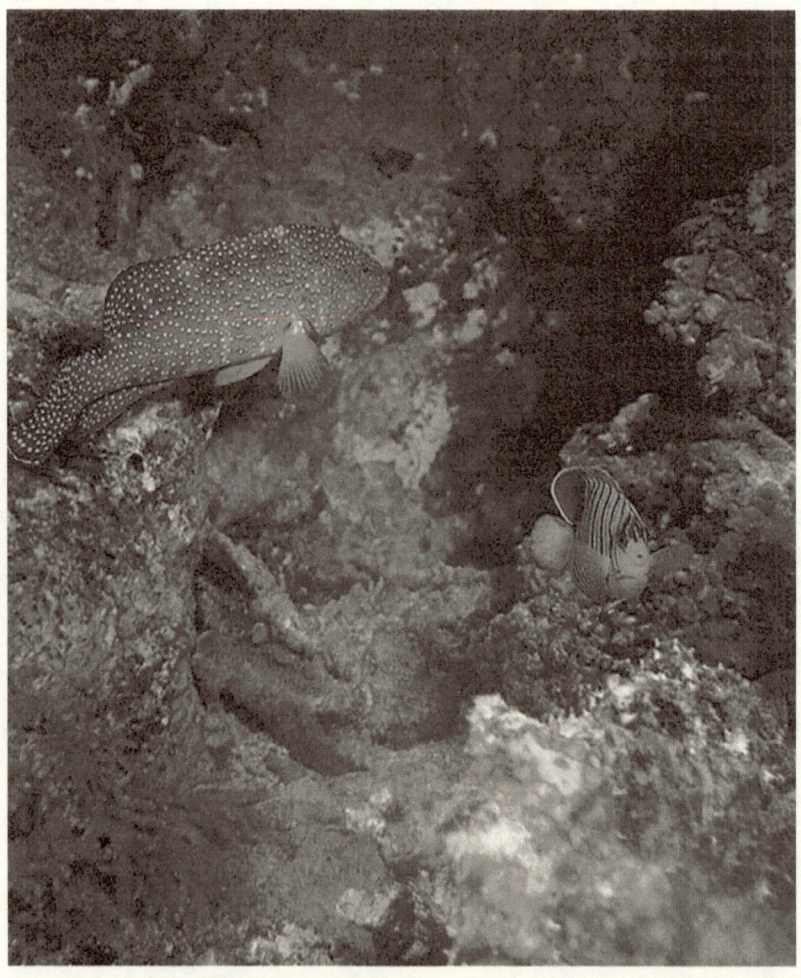

Even recalling this material puts me into a spiritual state. And I realized that our patterns of life repeat themselves from generation to generation.

To me, the small State of Israel has four very different worlds: the vast desert; the spiritual life of Jerusalem; the hectic and material life of Tel Aviv; and the forest in northern Israel. I suppose I could say this for any number of places; for example, Saint Patrick's Cathedral is a spiritual place within the frenetic physical life of NYC. However, in neither Manhattan nor Tel Aviv, do I feel - nor fathom - the vibrations I experienced while in the desert.

VACATIONING WITH GOD

Perhaps the most important, is the continuous change of the land; from swamp to farm land and from desert to fruited tree groves and parks.

We didn't spend time in Eilat – after lunch, the bus headed up to the Dead Sea. After a conventional adventure at the Dead Sea, we went back to Jerusalem.

NOTE:

I will discuss the continuous miraculous transformation of Israel's land from the beginning to today – and the day you visit the Holy Land, in Part II, Chapter 12.

David's Tomb

CHAPTER SEVEN
THE POWER OF STONE

TOUCHING THE STONE'S POWER
ADVENTURE NINE – KING DAVID'S TOMB

Located outside the Old City walls, we visited King David's tomb. (King David is actually buried in the Jerusalem of ancient times - now called the "City of David" - located on the southeastern hill in the Kidron Valley, south of the Temple Mount.) Regardless, when the Turkish Sultan Suleiman rebuilt the city walls in 1538, the King David's Tomb was mistakenly left outside the walls.

Inside the building, the monolith looked like the ones at the Tomb of the Patriarchs, except perhaps smaller. As a group, we entered the two-story high stone building and a Rabbi was giving blessings to people standing behind the stone.

According to our Rabbi, if you paid the man a few shekels, he would say a blessing for you. I cynically thought, even here in King David's holy burial place, money permeates the scene, and I was put off. However, everyone else in my group gave the Rabbi a few shekels and received his blessing. I was the last to leave, but conforming to the norm, I too, gave the Rabbi the required money. As he started his blessing, my eyes were wide open and wasn't in a prayer/meditative stance. I put out my left hand to touch the pillar and was hit by a large electrical shock, several times stronger than the shock received by static electricity. While the charge did not hurt me, it sure surprised me - what was going on?? No one else seemed to have received this shock; but on the other hand, no one else touched the monolith either.

The Last Supper

We left the building and went outside. I suggested to the group we venture upstairs and they asked why. I said supposedly that room was the location of Christ's last supper. No one else cared, so I climbed up the stone steps alone, to the second floor. Factually, the actual site of the Last Supper is not known, and the building of David's Tomb was built hundreds of years after Christ's death. Irrespective of location, it is interesting to note that the elements of the Eucharist are based upon the fact that bread and wine were served at the Last Supper.

The empty chamber was built of flagstone; carved gothic pictures lined the walls, appearing to be from the Middle Ages. I immediately thought the Teutonic Knights must have accomplished this task as the age of the drawings was certainly not of Christ's time. I sat down to meditate and pray. Nothing happened. Oh well, I thought, either this was not the room of the Last Supper or the shock I received downstairs in the tomb had neutralized my sensibilities, or…I just didn't know.

Like Mary's Well Adventure, the second part of this story occurred many years later while I was visiting the British Museum. During the reign of the British Empire when it controlled many parts of the world, its archeologists conducted countless number of digs. Some of the most magnificent antiquities and historical creations that man has ever produced, were brought back to England. England displays these phenomenal artifacts[19] in the British Museum and many of the countries of origin want them back.

Entering the room of the Babylonian relics, I passed under the two enormous gate guardians of Babylon made of stone. One statue had the body of a lion, wings of a bird and the head of a bearded man, while the other's body was that of an ox, also with wings and a bearded man's head.

VACATIONING WITH GOD

As I walked past, without thinking, I reached up toward the beard of one of the guardians, approximately 7 feet off the ground. I was hit by another electrical shock, as I had been in David's Tomb. Again, the charge was much stronger than static electricity discharge. I thought back: there was no carpet in David's Tomb, nor was there any carpet on the museum floor. What was this all about, I wondered?

Even today, after much research and scholarly wandering thru the religions of the east and the psychology of the west, I still lack an explanation.

I am thereby, left with a guess: these two entities, King David's Tomb and the guardian Winged Bull/Lions statues in the British Museum still maintain power. They represent people and gods that were powerful in their time, and are still able and willing to display their numinosity.

Last Supper

From the research in this book discussed in the Hebron experience, where the large stone tombs have no power; whereas, Rachel's tomb, Jesus' Star and King David's tomb have power, I believe they are authentic.

Of course, as discussed in this book, different objects have different vibrations (holographic remembrance), to different people. Something that may excite me, may not excite you, the reader/Pilgrim, and vice-versa.

VACATIONING WITH GOD

ADVENTURE TEN – THE WALL AGAIN

During the tour led by the Rabbi, we visited various interesting sites, schools and synagogues while in Jerusalem. My roommate Mark, wanted to visit the Wall as he hadn't been there before. I said I would be glad to join him, so we left on our own for another adventure.

We donned yarmulkes and approached the wall. We placed our heads and hand upon the rough stone of the wall and said separate prayers. When Mark removed his hand, a semi-large piece of the wall came off easily, almost rolling into his hand. "Look!" he cried; this was incredulous. I have never seen or heard of such an occurrence. This support wall of the Temple Mount was thousands of years old. Over time, it had been weathered, shot at, and yet, maintained its integrity. But here and now, Mark held an approximately 5 lbs. boulder-like piece in his hand.

Mark asked why. Without thinking, I replied, "do you remember back in Mt. Sinai a week ago, when the bad weather came in and the group descended? You chose to remain on the top and were willing to take your chances. Everyone else, including the Rabbi, went down. You faced Yad-Hey-Vav-Hey[20] on your own. You were unafraid and stayed on the top like Moses." I then laughed and said, "And you, like Moses, are Egyptian. The rock of the Wall is a personal gift to you from the Deity. Keep it and remember."

NOTE:

In this book, I have discussed adventures/unusual mystical experiences people have had at the wall, three different times. This is such a Holy place, where so many people (Jews and Non-Jews) experience something "other". I will try to explain what this phenomenon is about. The Western Wall, also known as the Wailing Wall or Kotel (Hebrew) is the foundation of the Holy Mount. Some Rabbis believe that when the Holy Temple was destroyed, Yod-Hey-Vav-Hey, (the unpronounceable name of God) took up residence in the wall. The wall was built to contain the Temple Mount and is 1,601 feet-long. A portion of it is in the Muslim Quarter and there are 17 courses located below street level. It is a common belief, that it was built in approximately, 19BCE by Herod, The Great.

The Wall is in and attached to the earth. It is part of the history of Judaism since the Jews, Christians and Muslims, believe that the Holy Templecontains the foundation rock where Abraham was going to sacrifice Isaac (the Muslims believe that Abraham was supposed to sacrifice Ishmael). Recent archaeological discoveries confirm the historian, Josephus Flavius who stated that the construction was finished during the reign of King Agrippa II, Herod's great grandson.

To the Jewish people, it represents their beginning. In order to understand the relationship of the Jewish people to the wall, I offer the following explanation:

I have talked to many Jews that have visited the wall, and most were overcome with emotion and it brought them to tears. It is interesting to note that the tough Israeli paratroopers that liberated the Wall in the 6-Day War in 1967, cried like children when they reached it and touched it. Most of these paratroopers are Jewish by tradition, but not religious. Many are secular and some Atheists... But they all cried.

In order to explain the emotional reaction and mystical experiences, I must become tutorial. The anthropologist, Levy – Bruhl, coined a term, "The Participation Mystique", in which he describes a relationship with an object, ("the thing" of power) in which the individual or subject cannot distinguish him/herself from this "thing". This is because there is an unconscious relationship between he/she and their culture. This relationship object or Holy artifact is connected when the individual is born. Carl Jung refers to part of this relationship that occurs between people, is the same with the "thing". A part of the personality is projected into the object and the object is then experienced with projected content. This became part of Jung's Collective unconscious, which I will try to explain in Part II of the book.

What is deeply interesting, since the Wall represents Judaism and it's basic Monolithic contents, since Christianity and Islam are a branch of the Tree of Judaism, we can visualize the Wall as being a deep root into the heart of the City of Gold – God's Chosen City. It represents Western Man's moral and ethical heritage. Therefore, we can explain why the American PHD (see page 11) who was a Christian, cried uncontrollably when visiting the Wall.

"THE WALL HAS POWER, VISIT IT, SO YOU CAN EXPERIENCE THE POWER."

If these stories of miracles and spiritual experiences with the wall that I have shared, intrigue you... I recommend you take the time to read a book called, "Talk To The Wall", written by Rabbi Dan Bloch. In this book he shares many more experiences with people and the wall.

Via Dela Rosa

Today

CHAPTER EIGHT
CHURCH OF THE HOLY SEPULCHER

ADVENTURE ELEVEN - CHRISTIAN FOR A DAY

After several more days in Jerusalem, including several side trips, I had a free day. This was my third or fourth trip to Israel and I felt comfortable wandering around alone in the Old City. I had bought some archeological treasures from a Palestinian shop that sold antiquities. (I had read that General Moshe Dayan bought antiquities from this particular shop so that's why I thought they were real, and now on display in my living room.)

I was wandering about the Old City, eating some of the vendors' wares, with a yarmulke on my head, feeling very Jewish, when I saw a group of Americans walking up the road toward me. A Minister was leading them in a single file, orderly fashion. I realized I was on the Via Dolorosa, where supposedly Christ had carried his Cross. Following his trial with Roman Pontius Pilate, Jesus was condemned to death, and traveled along the Via Delarosa on the way to his crucifixion. Also known as "The Way of Sorrows" or the Road to Calvary, Jesus carried the cross to a hill, of which the Church of the Holy Sepulcher was built upon. The route has 14 stations, each tied to events that happened on the way to the site of the crucifixion.

As the group approached me, I noted they were singing the 23rd Psalm, which I had heard in my own head only a week earlier on top of

Mt Sinai! I immediately realized that had been a sign for me to join this group on the Via Dolorosa. In addition, I understood that to prepare me for what lay ahead, it was vital for me to hear the 23rd Psalm.

> *The LORD is my shepherd I shall not want.*
>
> *He maketh me lie down in green pastures; He leadeth me beside still waters.*
>
> *He restoreth my soul; He guideth me in straight paths for His name's sake.*
>
> *Yea, though I walk through the valley of the shadow of death, I will fear no evil for Thou art with me;*
>
> *Thy rod and Thy staff, they comfort me.*
>
> *Thou preparest a table before me in the presence of mine enemies; Thou hast anointed my head with oil; my cup runneth over.*
>
> *Surely goodness and mercy shall follow me all the days of my life; and I will dwell in the house of the Lord forever.*
>
> *"If you do not see God, you will find God. God does not ask anything else of you, except that you let yourself go, and let God be God in you."*
>
> —*Meister Eckhard*

I joined in the singing. The energy of the group singing the Psalm and of me joining in, wedded me to them and I felt compelled to walk with them. Despite the yarmulke on my head, I was accepted. In that moment, I felt like a Christian, traveling Jesus' path with my brethren.

Finally, we came to the Holy Sepulcher, the most important Christian church in the world. At the urging of his mother (and mystic) Helena, Emperor Constantine built the church in approximately 330 CE. Just as she had divined Christ's birthplace in Bethlehem, Helena similarly fathomed the location of the crucifixion. Supposedly, she also found the actual cross upon which he had been bound within the walls of the rock of Golgotha. In Hebrew, this translates as "skull" - the little knoll where the crucifixion took place was rounded like a bare skull.

Upon reaching our destination, my group and I waited in the very long line, both inside and outside the building. Once inside the vulnerable church, we moved slowly until finally reaching the Holy Sepulcher, a small enclosed area where only a small group of people can fit at a time. As one person leaves, a priest allows another to enter. I noticed if anyone stayed more than a couple of minutes, the priest tapped their shoulder and moved them along.

I finally entered with last of my group, went to the far wall, sat down, prayed and meditated. The chattering of the crowd disappeared; I was in my own quiet space for a long time, perhaps an hour. So this is Christ's area, Christ's power - I felt no shock like I did at King David's tomb, but of course, there was no pillar to touch. Or, perhaps Christ's energy represents peace, not war.

From my reading of Josephus, Christ was a real person who lived in Bethlehem and preached love. He refused to be a warrior; at that time, many Jews wanted to revolt against the Romans. (This did not occur until 132 years later, known as the Bar Kokhba revolt, its leader Simon bar Kokhba prevailed over the Roman Empire for three years.) All of a sudden I realized the message of love does not have the power of warfare. There would be no shocks here, only quiet contemplation.

I entered a spontaneous altered state of consciousness – peaceful, ecstatic, comfortable, and my awareness expanded; and I thought when humans are born into this hostile environment, we feel abandoned by God. We quickly assume that our mothers and fathers, if we have them, are the Father God and the Mother Goddess, and if we are loved, we can have a loving life. As a contrast, for those with no loving parents, life becomes a fearful place, full of anxiety, problems and misfortunes. We all must learn to love ourselves.

Church of the Holy Sepulchre

Many people live in fear, and we strive to overcome it by gaining power, be it political, monetary, or physical. Having powers over others makes us feel safe. But using power inappropriately can be very detrimental to others, causing fear and/or pain. In these cases, we have traded off love for power. Christ never did. His message was to love your neighbor, your community, your God, and never abuse others for they are your brethren.

Interestingly enough, the priest never tapped me on the shoulder. Somehow, this man (who I never met before and will never meet again) and I established an unspoken trust. Though we didn't shared language or religion, we had a binding belief in the Deity. He with his belief that Deity/the method to communicate with the Deity, was with the Lord, Jesus Christ; Whereas I believed, as a Jew, I could communicate with the Deity, Yad-Hay-Vav-Hay (which the Christians instead, use the term, Jehova). At that time I did not know why he allowed me to remain. Perhaps he could sense I was in the middle of a numinous experience.

Years later while visiting a museum in Florence, Italy that housed artifacts removed from the great church of Florence (commonly known as the II Duomo di Firenze), I came upon a magnificent stone carving by Michelangelo, one of his pietas called the Deposition. The sculpture contains 4 figures: the dead body of Christ that was taken off the cross, being supported by the Virgin Mary on one side, Mary Magdalene on other side, a male figure, either Joseph (husband of Mary) or Nicodemus, from behind.

Going into deep meditation, I touched the stone at the lower leg of Jesus. I could feel tissue and bone underneath the stone leg. I have heard the statement Michelangelo could turn stone into flesh, and I was living proof of that statement. So I thought to myself Christ did live, and his messages of love are alive today for those who wish to believe.

JACK LIN

NOTE:

The New Testament states that Jesus was always Jewish and his gospel was intended for Jews and his followers were only preaching to the Jews and trying to help them understand Christ's message of love. Christ's notion of brotherly love is also the message of Hillel[21] who considered "love of man" as the kernel of Jewish teaching. Hillel summarized the 613 laws the Jews should follow into a simple but difficult conduct. When asked to provide a concise summary of the Jewish religion, he replied "What is hateful to thee, do not unto thy fellow man: this is the whole law; the rest is mere commentary."[22] It appears he is the father of the "Golden Rule."

Indeed, Christianity was not started by Jesus Christ, but by Saul Paul. The famous story of his enlightenment on the road to Damascus to the Greeks and Turks and he converted Christ's teachings into Christianity. He was converted from a simple Jewish tax collector to Saint Paul. He created Christianity through his life of performing sermons and writings letters.

The division between Jesus Christ's and Saul Paul's beliefs was so great, that when Saul met with Jesus's disciples, they did not get along.

That night as I reflected upon the day, I wondered why this experience was so different than the day I felt like a Muslim at Mt. Sinai. My logical mind quickly came to my aid. I was born in Canada, and at age 10 moved to the US where I have lived my entire life. The majority of the population in these 2 countries follows some branch of Christianity; thus, I live in a Christian collective. According to Carl Jung, the collective unconscious shapes much of our behavior although we are unaware of this process.

As a child in the Bronx, NY, I was hit over the head with a bottle and was bleeding profusely. My mother, an Orthodox Jew, had to take me to closest hospital, which happened to be Catholic. I knew she felt awkward and embarrassed, but I received excellent medical attention from the nuns. The population of the neighborhood in which I lived was over 90% Irish Catholic, which included all of my buddies and girlfriends.

So, I had significant exposure to Catholicism throughout my life and was surrounded by the consciousness of Christianity. All the Irish people in my neighborhood had emigrated from the County of Cork, so when

VACATIONING WITH GOD

I traveled to Ireland as an adult, visiting that County was high on my list of priorities. And, it also happens to be the location of the Blarney Stone, of which indeed I did kiss! I noticed that I felt at home in Ireland, as I felt at home in Israel, but did not feel when I traveled to England, France, Germany or Italy.

Jesus, of course, was always Jewish and his gospel was intended only for Jews. Saul/Paul took the message from his enlightenment on the road to Damascus to the Greeks and Turks and eventually, converted Christ's teachings into Christianity. Indeed, Christ's notion of brotherly love is also the message of Hillel,* who considered "love of man" as the kernel of Jewish teaching. When asked to provide a concise summary of the Jewish religion, he replied "What is hateful to thee, do not unto thy fellow man: this is the whole law; the rest is mere commentary." ** It appears he is the father of the "Golden Rule."

Thus, it was easy for me to feel like a follower of Christ without giving up my Judaism; being inside the Holy Sepulcher with my yarmulke on my head, I easily participated in the loving of Christ's gospel.

Regrettably, human beings have not internalized the message of love. Until a peace treaty was agreed upon in 1998, followers of two different sects of Christianity - Catholics and Protestants - terrorized one another in Northern Ireland.

Today in the Middle East, Muslims butcher Christians, but in greater numbers, they kill other Muslims. Unfortunately, a schism occurred in Islam from the very beginning of its inception that lead to tremendous conflict, warfare and intra Islamic killing.

Muhammed died but had not named a successor. Two separate denominations arose after his death in 632CE. Muhammad's close friend and father-in-law, Abu Bakr al-Baghdadi started the Sunni sect in Saudi Arabia, and he was backed by the majority of Muslims. However, a smaller group favored Ali Talib, Muhammed's cousin and son-in-law and argued that they he should be the successor due to a direct bloodline.

They were not successful and eventually developed into their own sect called Shi'a.

The war that eventually developed between the two factions has been violent with destruction and death and exists to this day. Most Shi'a live within Iran, Iraq, India and Pakistan. Most Sunni reside within Saudi Arabia Egypt and most other Muslim countries and compromise approximately 90% of world's Muslims.

The teachings of Christ and Hillel have fallen upon many deaf ears, to the detriment of all of us. "What profits a man if he gains the world and loses his soul."

CHAPTER NINE
MOUNT MORIAH AND THE DOME OF THE ROCK

TOUCHING THE STARTING POINT OF WESTERN RELIGIONS

The Holiest site in Judaism is the Temple Mount in Jerusalem. The Western Wall is a retaining wall of the Mount, and thus, the only physical place where Jews can go to pray which is left from the original Temple. Two of the great events in Jewish history occurred on the Mount. The first, called the Akedah, was the binding of Isaac by Abraham preparing to sacrifice his son per God's instructions, to prove his belief in God.

The second, some thousand years later, was that Solomon chose this location to build his Temple. Inside Solomon's Temple, a sacred room within a room called the Holy of the Holies, contained the stone tablets upon which God had etched the Ten Commandments given to Moses.

The Temple Mount is also holy to Muslims who believe this is the exact location from which the Holy Prophet Muhammad ascended to heaven. The Muslims also believe the Angel Gabriel took Muhammad to this exact spot to pray with Abraham, Moses and Jesus.

The Holy of the Holies, a perfect cube measuring 15x15x15 was God's special dwelling place amidst his people. A curtain-like veil shielded God from sinful man. Whoever entered the room was entering into the presence of God, and if anyone except the High Priest entered, they would die instantly. Even the High Priest could not enter except on one day a year, the Day of Atonement. To this day, Orthodox Jews will not go upon the Temple Mount, as it is believed God's energy still dwells in this location.

There are two well know structures on the Temple Mount. The first is the Dome of the Rock, the most recognized site in Jerusalem due to its golden dome. The second edifice is the Al-Aqsa Mosque.

VACATIONING WITH GOD

ADVENTURE TWELVE - DOME OF THE ROCK

I had joined a group that was about to visit the Dome of the Rock. We walked thru the Mount and entered the magnificent building. We walked down to the lower level to view the Foundation Stone, which is believed to be the rock upon which Abraham placed Isaac, and also believed to be earth's foundation (see Footnote #4, Chapter 4).

I milled around a bit, then I felt the need to meditate but there wasn't an appropriate spot. Not wanting to sit on the floor by myself, I remained a tourist and thought about its history.

It is believed that God had instructed Abraham to go to the top of Mount Moriah, and upon that Mount, sacrifice his only son Isaac. Since Abraham believed in God and God's miracles, he was willing to kill his son.

Abraham led Isaac, two servants and a donkey on a three-day march to Mount Moriah. Only he and Isaac walk to the top, where upon Abraham builds an altar, arranges wood on top of it, binds Isaac to the wood and then draws his knife. But an angel of the lord calls out to him to stop; God realizes Abraham fears and believes in him so the human sacrifice is unnecessary. At this point, Abraham spots a ram in the bushes and sacrifices the animal instead.

As I reflected upon the history of Abraham and Isaac, and the Holy of the Holies, nothing happened to me out of the ordinary.

I followed the group ascending up the stairs. Then something strange occurred. A drop of liquid fell from ceiling and landed on my forehead near my eye. My scientific mind attempted a logical explanation; surely it must be water. Yet, it had not rained in days.

Once outside and in sunlight, I put my finger upon the drop of liquid and brought it down to my eyes for inspection. It was bright red…could it be blood from the ram Abraham sacrificed? My mind raced, of course not, that would have dried up thousands of years ago.

Foundation/Sacrifice Stone

I then tasted the drop and it was salty. Maybe it was blood? I decided to forget about the incident as it was beyond my understanding.

While organizing and writing this book numerous years later, I reflected upon the drop and where it had landed on my face, which was by my eye. I now believe it was a teardrop from the power of Yad-Hay-Vav-Hay (Hebrew name for God). I wondered why the Deity needed to cry?

I then reflected on this place of sacrifice, animal and human (or, not human, as in the case of Isaac). I traveled to many part of the world to learn about sacrifice - from the Pyramids of the Sun and Moon built by the Aztecs in ancient Mexico, to the Fiji Islands and finally to Katmandu where human sacrifice existed until 1928 (and unfortunately, still occurs today in small villages[23]).

If we look to biblical interpretations, the Rabbis tell us God was testing Abraham: was he *willing* to sacrifice his son? (God never meant for him to complete the deed.[24]) All the Gods of that early era in human history demanded sacrifice. The elders would cast a newborn child (gender was dependent upon the gender of God) to death to appease the Gods. Thus, in Abraham's mind, the Deity was following the path of other Deities of his time and culture. Therefore, accepting this request was not an unfamiliar practice. However, the God of Abraham made a statement that he was different than the other Gods of the time; he sent down an angel to intervene before Abraham plunged the knife into Isaac.

The story of sacrifice is repeated within the Old Testament.[25] Abraham would have sacrificed a part of himself via sacrificing his flesh and blood; Samson sacrificed himself to defeat the Philistines; and David appeared to have been sacrificing himself by the use of a mere slingshot to combat the armored giant, Goliath.

Reflecting again on the drop of fluid, the teardrop from the Deity. I now believe, the Deity did not want to destroy humans. The Deity's covenant with Noah[26] reflects the Deity's intent. Yet for humans to have freedom, we became predators and destroyers. Even today in the 21st century, darkness persists in our souls. For example, young Muslim suicide bombers believe they will go to heaven by their murderous actions. These individuals are caught up in the powerful, yet negative, side of love for the Deity.

The story of Abraham and Isaac tells us that for the first time, the Deity could feel the intense anguish and overwhelming sorrow of a man/father who had to destroy his own son.

In a similar story, the Book of Job, the Deity tested Job's love for him. Job states he loves God and is a holy man of his age. Following the advice of Satan, the Deity tests Job and destroys his wife, children and material wealth. He asks God why did he do that to him, even as he sat on a pile of ashes. The Deity finally understood Job's message but could not explain to Job his imperfect process in his communication. Deity asks Job, did you create the world, the oceans? Job senses the power of God and therefore, says a few things to the effect of, "whatever you wish, I do. I have nothing before you. You are greater than beyond my ability to perceive."

Since we find a similar narrative in the Hindu's Bhagavad-Gita,[27] might this be a mystical revelation? In its most poignant story, Arjuna, a warrior and an Achilles-like figure, is to lead a battle against uncles and cousins. But Arjuna tells his Deity, Krishna he will not fight and puts down his weapons. Krishna tries to persuade him to attack; Arjuna then asks to see evidence of Krishna's powers. Krishna exhibits his power and divinity to Arjuna, in an equivalent way to how the Jewish Deity exhibited his power to Job. Arjuna then understands, and led his tribe into battle.

Carl Jung believes Job's story becomes the precursor for Christ. The Deity realizes that he cannot truly understand man without becoming one, thus, allows the birth of a man who is also a God. This being - Christ - possesses the psyche of a human and the psyche of the Deity. From a Christian perspective, the Akedah narrative is completed; Jesus Christ becomes the sacrificial lamb. Christ consciously chooses to sacrifice himself; from that point forward, only humans will kill humans.

VACATIONING WITH GOD

Approximately 1800 years after the Binding of Isaac, Jesus proselytized to the Jews his message from heaven, the concept that we are all one, and each of us constitutes one part of the whole. As such, we must always love one another as we love ourselves. Christians might understand the story of Christ in the following way. The Hebrews met, accepted and lived with God for approximately two thousand years prior to Christ. After developing for those two thousand years, mankind was ready now for the next Commandment. Christ's message was an enhancement and/or refined communication from the Deity to the people.

However, the Hebrews of that time didn't understand the message; they became warriors and instigated the Bar-Kokhba Revolt against the Romans. This did not bode well, and they suffered a terrible defeat that resulted in grave consequences beyond the soldiers' death. Namely, their homeland and Temple were destroyed, and their population was scattered all over the Roman Empire.

According to the Gospel, there is an additional message regarding sacrifice of Christ; the Deity is willing to sacrifice itself (in the body of Christ) to forgive man's sins and therefore, sacrifice of humans and animals is no longer necessary. Plus, without a Temple in Jerusalem, the location to conduct animal sacrifice vanished, and the Jews lost the ability to be atoned via animal sacrifice and priest forgiveness. Instead, they atone by asking forgiveness from the Deity and any person whom they have sinned against. Although Israel gained control of East Jerusalem and the Temple Mount after the 6-Day War in 1967, they didn't rebuild the Old Temple.

According to the Bible, the prerequisite of building another Temple is the birth of a perfect red heifer (with a host of biblical criteria) that would be sacrificed in order to dedicate the Temple. There is a small sect of Orthodox rabbis in Israel that are attempting to breed such a cow, and are training certain individuals to be the priests to oversee the sacrifice and building of the Temple.[28] In my opinion, this will never occur.

More progressive Rabbis believe the Temple is actually held within us. Psychologists will tell us that in order to move forward and take on a new psyche, we must sacrifice our old conscious and unconscious feelings and behaviors. In their place, we substitute healthier ways to experience emotions and behave that are more appropriate for growth and final enlightenment. We must reach for a higher self since many modern Rabbis believe that our body is now the Temple. In essence, we are the home of God; we are now the Temple.

The Deity had an awakening, not only as a man, but as a parent. As I sit here contemplating this adventure, I realize on a profound level, the Deity no longer demands sacrifice. Instead, man would sacrifice man. Regrettably, in this day of scientific achievement, of space travel, nuclear weapons and iPhones, mans' inhumanity to man continues unabated. Fear, not love, dominates. The message of Hillel, Christ, Muhammad, Buddha and Lao Tzu are only partially heard by man.

Yet, the message is universal, especially within Christianity, Islam and Judaism, as Abraham was the forefather to all three religions. Perhaps the energies generated in this region of the world are available to all, regardless of religious faith, and even to those who aren't religious.

The energy source of the Deity is alive and well in the holy city of Jerusalem. Neither pictures/movies nor mere words can explain it. One must travel there to expose your body and soul to this field of energy, and to feel the sunrise on the Mount of Olives, outside the Eastern Gate.

NOTE:

If we are perceptive, we can sense the Deity two ways. First, as nature, in which Hashem, (the Hebrew name) God sets up the universe, makes its laws, and then departs, leaving man to do with it what he may, giving him dominion over it. (This is hard to imagine so a similar concept would be a computer programmer designing and then inputting complicated programs and then letting the computer operate independently.)

The second way for us to touch the Deity is through our own actions, and then via an interaction/allowance of the Deity to act through us; miracles become the synchronicity of the deity knowing how and when to help us when we fumble through life. Thus, the Deity can feel our feelings if we allow this, and vice versa, if we are sensitive enough. We become the Deity, and our actions become the Deity's actions in this dimension. The Deity and we become one.

Those who do not believe in miracles call these events synchronicity or strange occurrences. As an example, water that receded from the Red Sea, allowing ancient Israelites to escape Egypt but then violently flowed back to drown the Egyptians, could have been due to a force of nature called a tsunami.[29]

Tectonic plate movements cause earthquakes; these quakes can trigger volcanic eruptions and/or tsunamis, also called seismic sea waves (Japan, 2008; Indonesia, 2005).

Since the geography of Italy and the Mediterranean and Aegean Seas are close to the boundary of two plates, there is a great amount of volcanic and seismic activity in this region. Tsunamis generated in this area can crash upon the coasts of the eastern Mediterranean Sea.[30] I believe it is indeed possible a tsunami was responsible for the successful exodus of the Jews from Egypt, and as such, was a synchronistic event.

There are great philosophical discussions whether the Deity creates these events or not. The well-known philosopher Spinoza[31] believed that all the events occur by natural law versus the hand of the Deity. Very religious Jews especially those study the Kabbalah[32] - believe that God ordained these events before creating the universe, and they occur in accordance with his law. Furthermore, I believe the Deity synchronizes the event in the 4th dimension so that the timing of the Israelites escaping Egypt via the Red Sea is related to the occurrence of a tsunami.

Unfortunately, the planet absorbs our shadow side or negative consciousness. These emotions turn into vibrations that upset the earth, and result in earthquakes, hurricanes, tornados and floods. Natural disasters are the earth's way of curing itself, and the destruction of human and animal lives is the cost.

JACK LIN

On the lighter side, the following story may amuse you:

"When I traveled to Italy, I noticed a common object in all the cities I visited: Rome, Venice, Florence and Naples. A red telephone was mounted on a side-wall of every major church. I asked a priest about the red phones and was told it was a direct line to God. I asked why there was no coin slot or mechanism for a credit card payment. The priest replied, 'Oh no, but if you wish to call, you must give the church a contribution of 10,000. American dollars, however it is tax deductible.' Several years later while visiting Israel, I noticed the same red phone in an alcove on the left side if the Wailing (Western) Wall, except this phone had a slot for coins. I located a rabbi, brought him over and asked about the phone's purpose. 'Oh,' he said, 'it is a direct line to God and it costs 25 American cents.' 'What!' I said loudly, 'in Italy it costs $10,000.' The rabbi replied "oh, here it is only a local call."

PART II

Israeli Boy Looking into the Future

PART II

REFLECTIONS AND ANALYSIS OF ISRAEL

PAST, PRESENT AND POSSIBLE FUTUTE
MIRACLES

In Part II, we view the Holy Land through the lens of group dynamics. While some of these experiences are personal, they are not first hand. They are included only to support the hypothesis upon which this book is based. In my opinion, the Deity is more available at this tiny portion of the planet than in any other place on earth, that I have experienced.

CHAPTER TEN
HISTORICAL CIVILIZATIONS

GOD TOUCHING THE PAST CULTURES

"Over 300 years ago King Louis XIV of France asked Blaise Pascal, the great French philosopher, to give him proof of the supernatural. Pascal answered: "Why, the Jews, your Majesty — the Jews."[33]

In this second part, I will attempt to describe why I believe, like Pascal, that the Jews and the State of Israel are a supernatural occurrence. The illustrious historian of the 20th century, Arnold Toynbee of Great Britain, author of a twelve volume set, *A Study of History*, stated according to his theory that civilizations have life cycles marked by rises and falls, that the Jews are an anachronism - they should have been buried in time and non-existent today. US-born historian Will Durrant, author of The Story of Civilization, could not classify the Jewish people so he ignored them completely.

Never in mankind's history has an ancient people, thrown out of their land for two thousand years, returned to claim the territory of their origins and established a country with the same religious beliefs and following the same traditions as their ancestors thousands of years past. Never before in history has a dead language (Hebrew) been reignited and spoken by millions of people.

Israel should not exist. It's miracle of existence will only be recognized hundreds of years from now. Most men do not realize the Deity's actions are always accomplished by mankind under its bidding, and that synchronicity of natural events sometime play into the narrative.

Toynbee's theory of civilizations appears correct on all accounts; yet the Jews are here among us. For example, Israel's war of Independence should not have been won by any standard. The soon-to-be Israelis were a group of ill-trained and ill-equipped individuals who fought the armies of five Arab countries simultaneously with rifles and homemade Molotov cocktails against tanks and artillery. Yet they emerged victorious.

Why is Israel so unique and special? I believe that the hand of God is upon the people and the land. Therefore, since the entire area is numinous, it is possible individuals of all religious backgrounds, and even the non-religious, can be afforded the opportunity to touch the supernatural.

Israel is the land of miracles, many of which are readily known - they have affected all of mankind. These include the exodus of the Jews from Egypt and the births, lives and deaths of both Jesus Christ and Muhammad. Chapter 12 will illuminate some lesser-known miracles that have occurred on Israeli soil.

The next portion of this chapter will be devoted to what transpired to some of the great civilizations of the past. For those of you who desire a more in-depth analysis, I suggest you read the magnificent summary, *Vanished Civilizations* by Reader's Digest Association (Yes, *that* Reader's Digest!).

The Ancients

We of the western world think of ourselves as the descendants of two great traditions – the religion of the Jews and the science/logic of the Greeks. Yet the ancient Jews were never a great civilization due to size and limited power; many historians today don't even considered them to be a "civilization." As an example, in *Vanished Civilizations,* the Hebrews

VACATIONING WITH GOD

are thrown together under the title, Phoenicians and Hebrews, and do not have their own status. Yet all of the civilizations that existed during the time frame of the ancient Hebrews, and the others who began before the Common Era (CE) have disappeared into history.

In some areas of the world, the ancient people never left their land, despite being conquered by other civilizations. Thus, the same DNA of those original people exist today in the modern population. But their customs, religious practices and their political or governing methodology has completely changed. Egypt is a prime example.

Egypt:

While we typically consider Egypt to be one of the oldest civilizations (which began approximately 3200 BCE), in actuality, that original empire no longer exists. Some period of time after Egypt became the great land of the Pharaohs and pyramids, the Hyksos, the Assyrians and the Persians later ruled over them. Finally, Egypt was conquered by Alexander the Great in 330 BCE and became part of the Coptic Church in 200 CE. Later, Egypt was completely absorbed by the great growth of Islam; the culture of Egypt today is nothing like the time period when Pharaohs ruled the land and practiced the ancient religion of the stars. Today, it is an Islamic country and part of the Muslim civilization.

Other Civilizations in the Middle East:

The Sumerians of Mesopotamia is one of the oldest, organized civilizations, and actually somewhat older than the Egyptians. The Sumerian City-states were founded approximately 3600 BCE; and defeated by the Amorites in 2000 BCE. Over the next thousand years, the Sumerian people vanished as they blended into the various Semitic peoples who had migrated into Mesopotamia.

The Phoenicians occupied Canaan, the land of modern day Lebanon and Northern Israel. They came into existence approximately 3000 BCE. Despite being invaded on numerous occasions, the Phoenicians kept their base religions but disappeared totally after the conquest of Alexander in 332 BCE.

Other great civilizations/empires of ancient times have come and gone; such as the Assyrians (1900-600 BCE) and the Etruscans, (800-200 BCE). The third king of the Persian Empire (550-330 BCE), Darius The Great, organized the vast empire by dividing it into provinces, each governed by a specific leader and linked his lands by roads. He also allowed the Jews to continue to rebuild their temple after disputes from neighboring areas are brought to his attention. Alexander the Great overthrew the Persians over a period of ten years through a series of decisive battles.

Greece:

In Greece, the Minoan civilization began approximately 3650 BCE and lasted until approximately 1400BCE, while the Mycenaeans (1600 – 1100 BCE) disappeared after the Dorians permeated the land. Even the great Greek civilization of Athens and Sparta that anchored the modern western world through its science, democracy, language, philosophic thought, education, mathematics, athletics, arts and architecture was conquered by the Romans in 168 BCE.

Italy:

At one time, the Roman Empire (31BCE – 476CE) was the most technologically advanced civilization known to man. As one example, they are responsible for one of the most important architectural discoveries in human history, the form of an arch. The Romans were the first to master arches as a stand-alone figures; prior use was only underground, utilizing the earth as the reinforcement. This allowed them to build longer roads, better aqueducts and larger buildings that still stand today. Additionally, the Roman Empire is considered to be perhaps the greatest political and cultural powers in history.

In 146BCE, the Romans finally destroyed Carthage and became the most powerful Mediterranean state. First, they expanded their powers into the rest of the Mediterranean. However, they were not satisfied; they eventually conquered Western Europe, including England by 150CE. In order to keep out the Barbarians from the north, they built Hadrian's Wall (aka the Roman Wall) in approximately 122CE as a defensive wall in northern England. Some of the Wall still stands today, just as do portions of the Great Wall of China.

The Western Roman Empire lasted approximately 500 years and was eventually overrun by the Barbarians. The Catholic Church is its only remnant and Italy today is nothing like the Roman Empire.

India:

The Indus Valley Civilization, also known as the Harappan Civilization existed from 3300-1300 BCE and extended from modern day northeast India into northwest Afghanistan and Pakistan. The collapse of this civilization began in 1800 BCE and was due to a variety of factors – drought, a decline in trade with Egypt and Mesopotamia, infectious diseases, interpersonal violence and immigration of new peoples into its lands.

In the region known today as India, the emergence of Hindus began as early as 800-200 BCE. During this time period, the Hindu states emerge, and the birth of Buddhism occurs in this land approximately 430-424 BCE and eventually expands out of India as it declines within India. To counter the influence of Greek civilization under the rule of Alexander the Great in 326 BCE, Chandragupta Maurya founded the Maurya Empire 321 BCE, 2 years after Alexander's death. He was the first ruler to unify India into one state.

The influx of Muslims and their resulting political power began approximately 1200 CE; 100 years later, Muslims begin their reign over the land and influence the evolution of Hinduism until 1750 CE. Additionally, the Sikhs and the Buddhists incorporate part of the Hindu beliefs.

Despite being unified into one State, India did not have kings nor a central government. A Maharaja, who was in essence a warlord, ruled each separate province. The arrival of the Europeans between 1400-1750 soon leads to India's colonial era, capping off with the British conquest of 1858 that ended the rule of the various Maharajas.

Finally today, after Gandhi led the Independence Movement of the last century, India has a totally different political and economic system than under past rulers. The Hindu caste system had been law for centuries; it stratified people into rigid hierarchical groups based upon occupation but it also completely impacted Hindu social and religious life. When India became an independent nation in 1950, caste discrimination was abolished. A quota system was put into place to allow the lowest in the caste hierarchy access to jobs within the government and education.

Although some Hindus of today believe in millions of Gods, the more enlightened believe in Vishnu and Shiva, but all believe in the Great Creator, Brahma. Despite being split (into India and Pakistan in 1947), undergoing political reform. They became a democracy which rejects the caste system, and the Indians of today are the closest to ancient Hindu beliefs. Many people still believe in the old customs and the Vedas - the body of texts that originated in ancient India and constitute the oldest scriptures of Hinduism. If we consider their current culture in totality, perhaps 25% of the ancient beliefs are still alive today. This is the only civilization of which we can make this claim.

Unlike the Jews, the Hindus were never driven out of their own homeland and dispersed to other regions. The Hindus of today not only follow their original traditions, but also do so in the land of their ancestors.

China:

The other great Asian civilization, China – started approximately 2000 BCE when it went from a primitive society to a slave society in its first dynasty, the Xia Dynasty. The next several hundred years saw the transition from a slave society to feudal society within many independent principalities. In 221 BC, the Qin Dynasty established the first centralized and multiethnic state. Soon thereafter, the Han Dynasty prevailed from 206 BCE - 220 BC and united the country even further. It was under this dynasty that Confucianism was embraced, and became the underlying ideology of all later dynasties until the end of imperial China. After Han, many different dynasties dominated the political and economic scene until the revolution in 1911. At some point during the first century of the Common Era, Buddhism reached China and during the second century, Taoism came into being. However, the original religions of Taoism and Confucianism, as well as the more animalistic religions have taken a backseat to Buddhism.

The revolution of 1911 overthrew the current dynasty and the county became a republic. In 1949, the communist revolution led by Mao Tse-tung annihilated the old religions and political systems. The communist party is an atheist institution and prohibits party members from practicing religion while in office. While religious movements were oppressed under Chairman Mao, his successors allowed more autonomy to the religious organizations.

Other Civilizations:

Meanwhile, the Americas experienced the rises and falls of the Mayan, Aztec and Inca civilizations, while the Saxons, Celts and Vikings all rose and then fell in Europe.

Outliers:

However, there are two remnants of past civilizations that did endure. First, the small sect of Zoroasters, who were kicked out of their homeland (Iran), exist today in Pakistan with their religious writings. Second, the torment and tyranny of the Tibetan culture didn't result in its entire annihilation; after being kicked out of Tibet, they now try to survive in India. In 1989, the Dalai Lama met with top Jewish rabbis/scholars at the Tibetan Learning Center in Manhattan to talk about survival:

> "We always talk of the Jewish people scattered in so many countries, speaking so many languages," the Dalai Lama said in English, sometimes seeking the right word from a Tibetan translator. "Yet the Jews keep their traditions. It is something very admirable."
>
> The Dalai Lama said he wanted to learn the Jewish "secret technique" of survival. He said his question was not religious and political leader of Tibet, went into exile in 1959 in the face of the Communist takeover. He now lives in Darmasala, India, one of the many places of Tibetan "diaspora."
>
> He compared the Tibetan diaspora to that of the Jews. Jews use the term to refer to their dispersal after the destruction of the Second Temple in Jerusalem in the year 70.
>
> "We have to learn from the experiences of our Jewish brothers and sisters," the Dalai Lama said.[34]

In 1934, Mordecai Kaplan wrote a monumental opus, *Judaism as a Civilization: Toward a Reconstruction of American-Jewish Life*. One of his realizations was:

> "...The world would not be as far advanced in knowledge if it were not for Greece, nor in government if it were not for Rome. But both nations, and others before and since, played their part in the progress of mankind, unaware of their function. They were unconscious instruments in the divine plan. Israel, however, stepped into history fully aware of the mission it had to perform, and was prepared to suffer the antagonism of the nations because of its loyalty to that mission. This consciousness of purpose made Israel the chosen of God in a far truer and deeper sense than the one in which we can apply that term to the other great historic peoples. Moreover, the very nature of the contribution which Israel made to the world's progress entitles it to be called the chosen of God in a sense that is unique. The idea of God is of greater importance to human welfare than science, art or government. Judaism's gift to mankind, monotheism, is truly a miracle.

VACATIONING WITH GOD

All those other civilizations, with their Gods, culture and holy texts, have disappeared. Yet, only that small group of people is still alive today, and they have kept their same God, beliefs and moral code, and practice the same religious rituals while wearing the identical garments as did their ancestors. Pascal was right; the Jews are supernatural.

The Deity, working thru the Jewish people, gave us monotheism. Today, over one half of all humans living are monotheistic branches of the "Jewish tree" (Christianity and Islam). Israel is the ground upon which that tree grows. This tree and this ground can be touched and felt by you, as a pilgrim today.

For me, it is vital to be bonded to the Holy Land. I have a small jug, purchased in Israel from an antiquities store, that contains Israeli dirt. I have a routine whereby I place my moistened finger into the dirt and then swallow the residue. This ritual keeps my connection to this source and power, despite living almost half way around the world, in Los Angeles, CA.

NOTE:

Observation: As I finished the adventures and reviewed them in my mind, I realize that I have now experienced Christian, Jewish and Muslim religious/spiritual/numinous experiences. I can now try to review and comment on them. How do we process experiences like this? How do we understand them? How many humans have them? I, like most people, try to ignore or forget them. This is because they do not fit or fall into our Western view of reality. So I will try to look at them from a religious perspective.

From a Jewish point of view, Jews have tried for thousands and thousands of years to understand their relationship with the Deity. The mystical system they use is call the Kabbalah. The practitioners of Kabbalah use two methods. The first and most common method is in a theology school. Here a religious, mystical teacher transmits the material for his students. The second method is the belief that an individual can have a direct experience with the Creator, using prayer, fasting and meditation. The individual can enter into a state of self-hypnosis/altered consciousness and receive direct insight/knowledge from the Creator. Therefore, there are many Jews that have experienced these types of spiritual adventures.

From the Christian point of view, they have the same direct experience with one major change, Jesus said' "I and the Father are one." John 10:30. Thereby, the mystical experiences from God become a direct experience from Christ. The goal of the Christian Mystic is to become one with Christ. Let us remember, that just like in Judaism, it is not to be focused on the experience, but to use these experiences to create a union with God. Mystical teachers such as John of the Cross speak of the sole union with Christ/God.

As for the Islam point of view, we recognize that Mohammed had a direct communication with God through visits with the angel, Gabriel. He became both a prophet and messenger of God. This tradition of direct communication with God came from the direct teaching of Mohammed (as one is to worship Allah, if you see him; if you can see him; surely, he sees you).

Rumi, (perhaps the greatest Sufi poet), states, "The Sufi is hanging on to Mohammed like Abu Bakr did. Sufis regard Mohammed as the perfect man that displays the morality of God.

CHAPTER ELEVEN
THE JEWISH CIVILIZATION

GOD TOUCHING MAN – THE PAST

The Jews:

The ancient Hebrews typically integrated as a small minority (less than 1%) population into various civilizations, both Christian and Muslim, who ruled their land. In the context of their small numbers, limited geographical territory and lack of power (other than the short reign of Solomon) many historians did not consider the Jews as a separate civilization.

> *Starting in ancient times, the Jews questioned their own viability upon being forcefully exiled from the land of Israel, as seen in Psalm 137:*
> *"By the rivers of Babylon, there we sat down, yea, we wept when we remembered Zion.*
> *We hanged out harps upon the willows in the midst thereof.*
> *For there they carried us away captive required of us a song; and they that wasted us required us mirth, saying, Sing us one of the songs of Zion.*
> *How shall we sing the Lord's song in a strange land?..."*

The Jews did not consider themselves as a civilization until Mordecai Kaplan's book Judaism as a Civilization was published in 1934. Kaplan builds upon Matthew Arnold's description of the difference between Hebraism and Hellenism. Kaplan believes that mans' cognitive processing had been raised by viewing Judaism holistically as a totality, versus just a religion, similar to what Arnold described, "As seeing things integrally and seeing them whole (in their totality)." Arnold believed that in the maturation of the human mind, we went from mythology to philosophy to science; and only now we are beginning to think holistically.

I agree with Arnold's theory of human minds evolving. I believe that by mankind serving the Deity, the human race marches forward and becomes more aware of the universe, and the Jewish people are an integral part of this process.

Seeing the Jews as a totality, we see 4500 years of culture, methodology and the development of ideas leading to their tremendous affect upon the Western World. They still maintain their own unique identity while being the forefather to both Christianity and Islam. Clearly, the Jews are the only civilization to last 4500 years. Today in Israel, people pray in the same way, eat the same foods and speak a language that was once dead. Only today, through the lenses of time, can we attest to the Jews' survival against all odds; furthermore, we have witnessed the rise of Israel, currently ranked the 8th most powerful county in the world. These unlikely phenomena certainly earn the Jews designation of being a civilization.

So why did the Jews continue to exist when all the other civilizations and people died out? Any Rabbi will tell you it was because the Jews took their God and their Torah with them. However, it can be said that the 10 Lost Tribes[35] took the same God and Torah with them, yet disappeared into history.

While the majority of Rabbis are very erudite about Jewish history, many do not possess the same wealth of knowledge regarding world history and other religions. They don't take into account that other vanished civilizations mentioned in Chapter 10, retained their own

Gods, religious ceremonies, writings, laws and histories. Despite the survival of their literature, the Greeks and Romans of today are vastly different civilizations and peoples than during antiquity. Only their ancient edifices exist today.

Despite their small numbers, the Jews have been the most persecuted, attacked, maligned and cursed peoples in the world. A new word was coined to capture these negative sentiments and actions: anti-Semitism. That the Deity allowed the Jews to survive thousands of years in hostile lands, and in some cases blending their bloodlines with the local peoples, is indeed a miracle. In theory, Toynbee and Durrant are right; the Jews shouldn't exist.

Section II started with a quote from Blaise Pascal. Why was Pascale so ardent in his belief? Because like Constantine, Pascale also had a numinous experience on, or related to, a bridge, which resulted in the belief in one God, and in those cases, the acceptance of the Christianity.

It is noteworthy that these two enlightenment stories, both connected to bridges yet separated by approximately 1300 years, would be anchors to my thought processes.

Other learned and intelligent men of that time period have also reflected on the Jews. In 1899, Mark Twain pondered that despite being hated, the Jews were so persistent within an article he wrote for Harper's New Monthly Magazine, entitled "Concerning the Jews."[36]

> "…The Jews consist but of one percent of the human race… properly the Jew, ought hardly to be heard of, but he is heard of, has always been heard of…The Egyptian, the Babylonian, and the Persian rose, filled the planet with sound and splendor, then faded to dream-stuff and passed away; the Greek and the Roman followed, and made a vast noise, and they are gone; other peoples have sprung up and held their torch high for a time, but it burnt out…The Jew saw them all, beat them all, and is now what he always was, exhibiting no decadence, no infirmities of age, no weakening of his parts, no slowing of his

energies....All things are mortal but the Jew; all forces pass, but he remains. What is the secret of his immortality?"

In 1908, Leo Tolstoy was quoted in the Jewish World periodical[37]:

"What is the Jew? What kind of unique creature is this whom all rulers of all the nations of the world have disgraced and crushed and expelled and destroyed; persecuted, burned and drowned, and who, despite their anger and their fury, continues to live and flourish? The Jew - is the symbol of eternity...He is the one who for so long guarded the prophetic message and transmitted it to all mankind. A people such as this can never disappear. The Jew is eternal. He is the embodiment of eternity."

Certainly, Hitler was aware of the Jews' history, and even contemplated the possibility of their indestructibility in Mein Kampf.[38] Yet he went forth with his Final Solution. Despite wiping out nearly 40% of the world's Jewish population, he and his Nazi party were destroyed. Today, the Jewish population has rebounded, and the State of Israel was born. (As an aside, it has been widely speculated that Hitler's paternal grandfather was Jewish. Supposedly, the adult son of a Jewish couple who employed Hitler's grandmother as a cook impregnated her, resulting in the birth of Hitler's father, Alois. However, there has been no evidence found to support this claim.[39])

Thinking of the Jews as proof of the supernatural, Pascal pondered their survival. He stated "This people are not eminent solely by their antiquity, but are also singular by their duration, which has always continued from their origin till now...in spite of the endeavors of many powerful kings who have a hundred times tried to destroy them."[40]

Thomas Newton (1704-1782), the renowned British cleric and Bible scholar who served as Bishop of Bristol, declared in one of his sermons:

The preservation of the Jews really is one of the most signal and illustrious acts of divine Providence...and what but a supernatural power could have preserved them in such a manner as none other nation upon earth hath been preserved."[41]

For over forty years, I have pondered the following questions: Why was Zionism successful/why does the modern and dynamic State of Israel exist? Why was the renowned historian Toynbee incorrect? Why did the Jews survive while all other great civilizations perished in their own soil? Today, I received an answer.

Earlier, I had attended a Torah class being taught by a Rabbi. While discussing why the Jewish people were special, he pointed out that the actual number of Jews present with Moses at Mount Sinai was immaterial. Instead, the Jewish people as a whole directly received God's message.

Surely, the Deity had met and enlightened many humans during 8000 years of civilization, in addition to scores of primitive man leading to the development of tools and the ability to control fire. But it struck me that at Mount Sinai, the only time in world history, a whole people received the Deity. The Deity had infused their DNA so that later mankind such as David, Christ and Muhammad could also be enlightened. It is this energy that has kept the Jewish people – maligned, persecuted, exiled – alive and allowed them to create the State of Israel. And, we can expect more spiritually enlightened people to come forth in the future.

The Schism

Looking back at history from our modern-day perspective, we can see it holistically. Whether or not the Jewish people were a civilization, it is obvious they have been an integral part of Western Civilization, which is being tested today by Islamic Civilization. As everyone knows, there is a great dissonance/ disharmony between these two civilizations.

While the Western world exponentially transformed over the millennia, Islam has struggled with any deviation from the Koran. Since the world has shrunk driven by the speed of communication and transportation - the amount of interaction between these two very different civilizations has increased dramatically over the past 50 years.

And therein lies the problem: the ever-present butting up against one. The breaking point will be whether mankind continues to change, or will it shift and choose to stand still. But how did the schism occur in the first place?

For thousands of years, the Jewish people have argued over the Old Testament (the Torah), trying to ascertain its true meaning. As Christians witnessed this process, their theologians in turn picked up the tradition of debating God's true meaning behind the words. In Christianity and Judaism, the intellectual wrestling between religious scholars led to the development of logic and applied reasoning, which then allowed for a more modern-day change to the original traditions and doctrines.

The growing reliance upon logical reasoning led to the tremendous growth of Western Civilization, which flourished during the Renaissance. Many Sinologists[42] wonder why didn't the Renaissance occur in China considering their many great inventions (papermaking, moveable-type printing, gunpowder, the compass, clocks, tea and harvesting silk), most of which occurred centuries prior to the Renaissance. It was because the Chinese didn't develop logic. By developing applied reasoning and logic, the West could analyze the natural world to see how it came into being and evolved. Changes began to occur in all facets of life, and the Church was forced to change with the times.

In the intellectual and sociopolitical development of mankind, the Renaissance was a true paradigm shift; the way humans thought and interacted in the world completely changed. This time period spurned the Industrial and Scientific revolutions. The Europeans suddenly had a tremendous amount of power so they began to take over (e.g. colonize) territories all over the world map. This, in turn, caused different civilizations to interact and affect one another. A tiny example is the popularity of yoga and meditation in the US. Finally, during the past 100 years, we have achieved phenomenal scientific achievements…yet we are left with a shadow: weapons of mass destruction.

Unfortunately, Islam did not go through this process; the Koran has not been reinterpreted, as have both the Old and New Testaments.

VACATIONING WITH GOD

Fundamentalist Muslims who ascribe to Sharia Law believe they have no obligation to change just because the rest of the world has done so. (It is interesting to note, however, that they have been keen to adapt and avail themselves to modern technology while casting aside human rights and freedoms.) This huge gap between cultures is strikingly vivid in Israel. The vastly different lifestyles of the Palestinians versus the Israelis are literally side-by-side and visible to all.

Miracle 1

At Military Academies, Like West Point, instructors view past wars and examine the strategies, actions and methodology of opposing forces. They try to explain to their students, (Cadets that will become officers in the future) how a General/Commander made a different decision that could have changed a critical battle, such as Gettysburg. Had different decisions been made, the South could have won the battle, but they lost. This lead to the eventual defeat of the Southern armies and the surrender by General Lee.

In many of these wars, the sides were mostly even. Events and decisions could have changed their outcomes. In some wars, only one side could win because the odds were overwhelming. As an example; when the German Blitzkrieg, of Poland occurred, there was no way the heroic Polish officers on their horses could have defeated the German tanks and their air power. The state of Israel, winning the revolutionary war is equivalent to the Polish horsemen overcoming the German tanks. It couldn't happen but it did.

When one evaluates the Revolutionary War in 1948, when Israel was attacked by three countries and their sophisticated armies, the Israelis did not have tanks, large cannons or anti-tank guns at their disposal and should have been wiped out. Israel's main army consisted of farmers and refugees armed only with rifles and Molotov cocktails. This war has been described in many books (There is no need to describe it here).

In the 6-Day War, Israel was threatened by all of the Arab Nations, consisting of 5 sophisticated armies, armed by the Soviet Union. Their tanks and planes were the latest Soviet technology and they were outnumbered by 5 to 1. Israel had a total of 200 combat aircrafts, compared to Egypt, alone, had 1,400 MiGs. Comparing size, it would be the state of New Jersey against the rest of the United States. In manpower, it is estimated that it was 650 to 1. Again, Israel won this war. (I will not describe this war, as there are many books that go into great detail about this battle.)

As described in Chapter 11, The Jewish people should not exist, but they do; Israel should not exist, yet it does.

My message to the vast majority of Westerners is this: to understand yourself and your culture, you must visit Europe in order to see the history of how Western Civilization came into being… But to find its moral, ethical and spiritual core, and hopefully, meet your Deity, you must visit Israel.

NOTE:

In this chapter I only discuss 1 miracle. In the next chapter, I will discuss 11 more. However, the miracle of the creation of the State of Israel by the Jewish people is far greater than all of the rest.

CHAPTER TWELVE

PART A
MIRACLES

GOD TOUCHING MAN – THE PRESENT
MIRACLES 2 – 12

"Who will prefer the jingle of jade pendants, if he has heard stone growing in cliff?"
- Loa-Tsu

Miracle 1. Jewish People Survival and Creation of the State of Isreal

Israel:

So why did the maligned and cursed Jews not disappear like all the others? My belief is that as David had the hand of God on him, so do the Jews. And the greatest miracle, superior than the parting of Red Sea, or the overnight death of 185,000 Assyrian soldiers attacking Jerusalem (after the Deity told King Hezekiah thru the prophet Isaiah that Deity would save them), was the return of a scattered people to a land after 2000 years and re-establishing their culture, their religion, their language. Looking back throughout world history, there is nothing even close to this massive and astounding marvel.

Throughout recorded history, documented miracles have occurred in Israel. Scrutinizing both Old and New Testaments, the WebBible Encyclopedia has documented 124 miracles,[43] most of which occurred in Israel. Other theologians report slightly different numbers, but suffice it to say that many dozens of miracles are described in the Old Testament, and many more dozens are described in the New Testament.

Miracle 2

In modern times, miracles still occur in Israel. An example: *"A Miracle on an Israeli Bus,"* published in *The Times of Israel* by Esor Ben-Sorek, describes an occurrence on an Israeli bus over 60 years ago.

> "It was a very hot day in July 1951. I was in Tel-Aviv and too hot to walk. I boarded the Dan Bus #4 on the corner of Ben-Yehuda and Gordon streets. The bus was very crowded and there was no available seat. I had to stand next to a Yemenite woman holding a live chicken under her apron.

...As we approached another bus stop (I cannot remember which corner), three or four new passengers boarded.

When one evaluates the Revolutionary War in 1948, when Israel was attacked by three countries and their sophisticated armies, the Israelis did not have tanks, large cannons or anti-tank guns at their disposal and should have been wiped out. Israel's main army consisted of farmers and refugees armed only with rifles and Malotav cocktails. This war has been described in many books (There is no need to describe it here).

In the 6-Day War, Israel was threatened by all of the Arab Nations, consisting of 5 sophisticated armies, armed by the Soviet Union. Their tanks and planes were the latest Soviet technology and they were outnumbered by 5 to 1. Israel had a total of 200 combat aircrafts, compared to Egypt, alone, had 1,400 MiGs. Comparing size, it would be the state of New Jersey against the rest of the United States. In manpower, it is estimated that it was 650 to 1. Again, Israel won this

VACATIONING WITH GOD

war. (I will not describe this war, as there are many books that go into great detail about this battle.)

Miracle 3

From the Gaza Strip, the terrorist organization Hamas has fired over 10,000 missiles into Israel from 2006-2016[44], yet, the actual amount of Israeli civilian causalities is very, very low. What accounts for this? A sparsely populated area into which most of the rockets have detonated? Or that a large number of these unguided projectiles could not accurately be directed at specific targets due to inferior technology and lack of money? Many – even Hamas itself - believe the hand of God is involved:

> "The Talmud Yerushalmi tells us that in no way are we to depend on miracles. It argues that we must not desist from our obligations and must not wait for miraculous intervention from the Supernatural. How perfectly relevant are both of these views today. We witness hourly miracles. As one of the terrorists from Gaza was reported to say when asked why they couldn't aim their rockets more effectively: 'We do aim them, but their God changes their path in mid-air.' Amen! And when our God is not busy doing that, He is ensuring that the high-tech brain power of our 'start-up nation' is working overtime to produce yet another Iron Dome battery to help protect our cities and us."[45]

For a discussion on the notion of miracles, and descriptions of other Israeli miracles, please read the ***Notes*** at the end of this chapter.

Don't just take my word for it – listen to the highly intelligent Mr. Spock narrate the movie *"The Miracle of Israel"* which connects the strange and seemingly supernatural events surrounding the Jewish State's founding and survival over the last 68 years.[46]

Miracles can also be subtle and plain, a part of our everyday life. Yet, we don't see them as such. The great American poet Walt Whitman makes this abundantly clear in his poem, *Miracles:*

"Why, who makes much of a miracle? As to me I know of nothing else but miracles. Whether I walk the streets of Manhattan, Or dart my sight over the roofs of the houses toward the sky, Or wade with naked feet along the beach just in the edge of the water...To me, every hour of the light and dark is a miracle, Every cubic inch of space is a miracle, Every square yard of the surface of the earth is spread with the same, Every foot of the interior swarms with the same. To me, the sea is a miracle, The fishes that swim – the rocks – the motion of the waves – the ships with men in them, What stranger miracles are there?[47]

Over 100 years ago, God re-gathered his people from all four corners of the earth; early Jewish settlers driven only by faith came back to the land of their ancestors. The early soon-to-be Israelis – called Zionists – set up kibbutzim, cleared swamps, planted trees and revived the dead language of Hebrew, in addition to restoring the land. These Zionists were instrumental in helping many Jews flee from the Holocaust and migrate to Israel. Even after WWII, but before the establishment of Israel, many Jews fought their way past the British and clandestinely made their way to Israel.

The fact that this little country has been victorious in wars that they should not have won, against much larger and better-equipped armies of hostile neighboring countries is the MIRACLE OF ISRAEL.

This brings to mind another country that was miraculously victorious in a war it should not have won – our own United States of America.

United States:

In my opinion, there is another miracle, just as astonishing: the birth and creation of the United States of America. The creation of the US affected the culture of the entire world. One by one, many monarchies disappeared and were replaced with different types of democracies. Additionally, the US pioneered the concept of free enterprise, private property and the pursuit of a profit for everyone. Previously, all wealth stayed under the control of the kingdom and aristocracy. George Washington said that without Providence, the United States would not

VACATIONING WITH GOD

exist. As an American Jew and US Air Force Officer (ret.), both America and Israel are my countries. God created them, and despite great wars, God held them both together and continues to bless them.

As Americans, most of us are unaware of a few small pieces of history that occurred during the Revolutionary War. Just as the State of Israel was able to defeat much larger and better-equipped armies, the fledgling American revolutionaries somehow defeated the most powerful army of its time, the British Empire. It is my belief, along with George Washington's, that Divine Providence was more than just instrumental in the US victory. Three miracles in 1776 kept the American dream alive.

United States Miracle 4

The first occurred during the battle of Boston in March 1776. Previously, Benedict Arnold and his Connecticut militia captured Fort Ticonderoga in NY; this resulted in the obtainments of all its armament, most notably cannons, which were transported, miraculously, in the middle of winter, to Boston. Washington formulated a plan to force at least some of the British out of Boston by the use of this heavy weaponry and launch an invasion across the Charles River. During the unseasonably clear night, the Colonial soldiers dug trenches on the high grounds. They then had to fortify them with cannons for the upcoming battle. This would have been very loud and probably would have been noticed by the British on a nearby hill. Amazingly a rainstorm started and the sound from the rain muffled the sound of the cannon's movement. The British were greatly surprised by the amount of overnight progress and began to contest the move but the weather again dramatically shifted from clear to a severe storm. As a result, the British retreated from Boston within two weeks. Washington attributed the storm to the intervening hand of God.

United States Miracle 5

A second miraculous, abrupt change of weather occurred during a summer battle in New York. By sheer numbers, 30,000 British soldiers should have been victorious over 18,000 Continentals and militiamen in the Battle of Long Island. Indeed, as the British crossed from Staten Island into Brooklyn, they inflicted heavy losses upon the revolutionaries and could have crushed the smaller army. However, they did not move quickly enough and a rainstorm enabled Washington's troops to escape northward across the Hudson into New Jersey and then south to the Delaware River.

United States Miracle 6

The third miracle, an event known to all Americans, is Washington's famous crossing of the Delaware on Christmas Eve, 1776. We all remember pictures of him standing up in rowboat but the story is far more interesting.

America was on the verge of defeat; the number of troops was down to only a few thousand, and half of them were quitting at week's end as their enlistment was over. But Washington took a chance on one final offensive:

"…He gathered the same fishermen who had helped him retreat in August from New York and had his beleaguered troops ferried across the half frozen Delaware at midnight on Christmas Day. When daybreak came, their movement was covered by the elements, so the British never saw or heard their movements on the river.

Washington landed near Trenton in a blinding snow and hailstorm that served as a cover for his crossing and approach. His men quickly surprised a detachment of 1,200 Hessians. Colonel Rhal and his men had been partying and drinking with a pompous, false sense of security late into the night.

When Washington attacked in early morning almost all were captured and Rhal was mortally wounded. That day, Washington re-crossed the river with over 1,000 prisoners, and only 5 casualties of his own. As was his custom, he did not mistreat his prisoners.

The Americans immediately crossed the river again avoiding the massive British counter attack and surprised the British from the rear at Princeton. General Washington won another victory, riding his horse between the lines of fire and miraculously remained unscathed as both armies volleyed.

His troops rallied for a final charge and won. These victories changed the course of history. Almost all of the American soldiers re-enlisted. France began to support the cause, and hope in the providence of God (the great equalizer) reinvigorated the colonists..."[48]

Washington Crossing The Delaware M.M. of Art - Emanuel Leutze

George Washington believed that only by the grace of providence did the US win the Revolutionary War:

> *I am sure that there never was a people who had more reason to acknowledge a divine interposition in their affairs than those of the United States; and I should be pained to believe that they have forgotten that agency which was so often manifested during the Revolution, or that they failed to consider the omnipotence of that God who is alone able to protect them. He must be worse than an infidel that lacks faith, and more than wicked that has not gratitude enough to acknowledge his obligations.*[49]

Like the Israeli War of Independence, the US War of Independence should never have been won. But why do I bring this up? Jewish involvement. The first Jews to arrive in America, starting in 1654, were Sephardic, the lineage of the Jewish people persecuted by the Spanish Inquisition in 1492. Due to being as second-class citizens in Britain, many Jews chose to emigrate to Colonies throughout the 1700s where the rights afforded to them were far more plentiful.

In Pennsylvania, the Jews were fairly prominent and treated as equals. Their representation helped usher forth the freedom of religion that is taken for granted today. But back in the 18th century, this was not the case throughout the world. It was only in fledgling United States of America that Jews and those subscribed in other religions were given equal rights to practice their faith. Thus, alongside Christians, the Jews fought in Washington's army as soldiers and officers. However, the Jews' financial assistance to the war effort was of far more importance.

The oldest Synagogue built in 1759 for a congregation established in 1658, still stands in Newport, RI, and there were other established Jewish communities in the South. The Jews became zealous supporters of the American Revolution. They desired equal economic opportunity and freedom of religion.

They actually helped finance the American Revolution; in particular, immigrant Haym Salomon - along with Robert Morris,

VACATIONING WITH GOD

(the Superintendent of Finance) - was a prime financier. Salomon also strong- armed Jewish worshipers into turning over hard earned wages to the cause. In addition, many Jewish wholesale merchants provided gunpowder, lead, clothing and other equipment to the American army. Additionally, Jewish privateers, including Morris' ships, harassed British shipping.

Perhaps most importantly, Jewish arms traders and merchants helped to funnel arms to the colonies from the small free trading Dutch island of St. Eustatius, and had turned the island into a major arms center to support the American Revolution. This endeavor ultimately led to the British downfall in a roundabout way.

In 1781, the British realized they needed to stop this supply of arms from St. Eustatius. Admiral Sir George Rodney captured the island with the intent of destroying not only the supply line but also the whole merchant class. In addition to the demolition of arms and warehouses, Rodney had every Jewish home, and the synagogue, torched. Additionally, they confiscated Jewish property and imprisoned the merchants.

The many months spent at St. Eustatius proved to be catastrophic to the British position. The British fleet on the east coast was short in supplies and ships. Lord Cornwallis had retreated to a small port in Virginia, and was awaiting provisions. A small British fleet was sent by Rodney, but they were easily defeated by a large French fleet under De Graves. When the British army arrived in Yorktown, Virginia, they were up against the combined force of the French fleet, French army and the American army. They were trapped and had nowhere to go and were soundly defeated. This defeat caused the British to end the conflict.

It appears that God's hand on the Jews enabled Washington to defeat Great Britain, most powerful nation on the globe at that time. The Jewish efforts, energy and money became the "providence" by which Washington attributes to the victory.

In the years after the war, George Washington wrote to various Jewish communities; he assured them of religious freedom and thanked them for their good wishes:

To the Savannah, Ga., Hebrew Congregation
[14 June 1790]

Gentlemen,

I thank you with great sincerity for your congratulations on my appointment to the office, which I have the honor to hold by the unanimous choice of my fellow-citizens: and especially for the expressions which you are pleased to use in testifying the confidence that is reposed in me by your congregation....May the same wonder-working Deity, who long since delivering the Hebrews from their Egyptian Oppressors planted them in the promised land—whose providential agency has lately been conspicuous in establishing these United States as an independent nation—still continue to water them with the dews of Heaven and to make the inhabitants of every denomination participate in the temporal and spiritual blessings of that people whose God is Jehovah.

G. Washington[50]

On August 17, 1790, Washington visited Newport, Rhode Island; representatives of various religious denominations and leading citizens read letters of welcome to the President. A day later, Washington responded to the letter written by Moses Seixas, an official of Yeshuat - the first Jewish congregation in Newport - which expressed the Jews' happiness in Washington as a leader and in a democratic government which assured them of equal rights.

VACATIONING WITH GOD

August 18, 1790
Gentlemen:

While I received with much satisfaction your address replete with expressions of esteem, I rejoice in the opportunity of assuring you that I shall always retain grateful remembrance of the cordial welcome I experienced on my visit to Newport from all classes of citizens.

The reflection on the days of difficulty and danger which are past is rendered the more sweet from a consciousness that they are succeeded by days of uncommon prosperity and security.

If we have wisdom to make the best use of the advantages with which we are now favored, we cannot fail, under the just administration of a good government, to become a great and happy people.

The citizens of the United States of America have a right to applaud themselves for having given to mankind examples of an enlarged and liberal policy–a policy worthy of imitation. All possess alike liberty of conscience and immunities of citizenship.

It is now no more that toleration is spoken of as if it were the indulgence of one class of people that another enjoyed the exercise of their inherent natural rights, for, happily, the Government of the United States, which gives to bigotry no sanction, to persecution no assistance, requires only that they who live under its protection should demean themselves as good citizens in giving it on all occasions their effectual support.

It would be inconsistent with the frankness of my character not to avow that I am pleased with your favorable opinion of my administration and fervent wishes for my felicity.

May the children of the stock of Abraham who dwell in this land continue to merit and enjoy the good will of the other inhabitants– while every one shall sit in safety under his own vine and fig tree and there shall be none to make him afraid.

May the father of all mercies scatter light, and not darkness, upon our paths, and make us all in our several vocations useful here, and in His own due time and way everlastingly happy.

G. Washington[51]

From this start, the United States has grown to be the richest and most powerful nation on earth with freedom as its basic driver. America is an idea, as well as a nation. As is Israel, is an idea and a nation. The United States changed the world from kings and dictators who ruled over their subjects, to democratic governments with laws and freedom for their citizens.

As I look back at American history, we have had many great men and women in our beautiful country, but never have we had so many living at the same time in history. It is astounding to think about the vast number of intelligent and courageous men that were alive during the time of the American Revolution. This can be compared to the Greek scholars looking back at Greece's Golden Age.

The list of these American heroes seems endless, but here are some that stand out: Benjamin Franklin, George Washington, Alexander Hamilton, John Adams, Patrick Henry, Nathan Hale, Andrew Jackson, Paul Revere, Thomas Jefferson, Samuel Adams. All these men had European bloodlines, however, the greatest of all of them, Thomas Jefferson did not. Interestingly, he had a Middle Eastern bloodline.

The State of Israel – Miracles

Today, we witness the small State of Israel growing while under great negative pressure from its neighbors. When an American travels to Washington DC and visits historical sites – e.g. the Lincoln Memorial –

VACATIONING WITH GOD

it is possible to receive a spiritual revelation. But due to our materialistic culture, most of our spirituality has vanished. To touch the heart of mankind's mystical adventure, go visit Israel. Visit the Holy Sepulcher, Mary's Well, Rachel's Tomb and the Western Wall. The energies are alive and well, and waiting for you to taste them.

Miracle 7

Indeed, the entire state of Israel is a miracle. During the 6-Day War a massive miracle occurred. King Hussein, of Jordan had the duty to protect the city of Jerusalem and the Holy Shrines of the Muslims. However, as the tension was building up prior to the war, he began to receive pressure from his Arab neighbors. Sensing that war was now likely, King Hussein aligned Jordan with Egypt, suggesting an Egyptian-Jordanian Mutual Defense Treaty and the treaty was signed. The treaty stipulated that Jordan's forces were to be placed under the command of Egyptian General Abdul Moneim Riad (Like Eisenhower in WW II).

His loyal duty (which cost him his life) was to protect the city of Jerusalem. During the war, the Arab Legion starting shelling Jerusalem, as a prelude to a major attack. The Israelis counter-attacked by attacking all of the Heights above the city. With extremely bloody battles, Israel won these battles. One platoon lost half of their members in one night. The Arab League was trained and lead by British Officers and fought well. They could have continued fighting in Jerusalem, however, miraculously, General Riad had other ideas… He wanted a more defensive position so he ordered the Jordanian troops to leave the Old City of Jerusalem. King Hussein was powerless.

The Israeli paratroopers were assigned to defend the Old City, but much to their surprised, as they entered the Lion's Gate, they found no opposition. Because the paratroopers were young men, they had never been to the Wall because Jews were excluded for 19 years, so they were not able to find it. They received directions to the Wall by an Arab Gatekeeper, who said they he had been expecting their arrival. He opened the gate and let them in. as they came upon the Wall, these tough hardened men (most secular and non-religious Jews) cried openly and profusely.

Why do we cry so profusely at the Wall? In my opinion, we cry because we feel the Wall's energy, which is the Deity's reflection/projection into us. Without realizing it, we go deep into our Collective unconscious and we remember when are at oneness with the Deity. This is like having a dream, but we are fully awake. When we are born into this body-life, we lose our Heavenly existence. From this Holy Wall's energy; the energy of the Deity, we remember when our soul was a microcosm of the Deity. In that state we existed in love, unity, perfect harmony, peace and security, being a finite part of the Deity/Universe.

When we were born into our bodies, we felt abandoned by God, and infinite loss. He deserted us to the fear-filled life. In this life-form we are made to want to survive, which creates a fear of death in this existence. At the place, this Holy massive Wall we are overcome by our feeling of loss. However, since these feelings are in our Collective unconscious, we are unaware of this and therefore we cry and do not understand why. This explains why my roommate, the Christian PhD (see chapter 11) cried so uncontrollably when he visited the Wall.

If you might be thinking this explanation is too bizarre, there is an understanding that this Wall is different. When you hear expressions like, "Some men have hearts of stone and some stones have hearts of God" or "Walls have ears", it is believed that these were created with this Wall in mind.

NOTE:

Miracles shouldn't happen in our technological, materialistic Western society. The supernatural is usually presented as a bag of tricks by a magician in Las Vegas using mirrors and trap doors. Yet many things that should not have occurred due to the odds being stacked against it indeed do happen. There is a term for it; we call it a "strange occurrence." Sometimes it is a confluence of events leading to a perfect storm. Even very simple or basic things can be thought of this way.

VACATIONING WITH GOD

An example: to our naked eye, the moon and sun appear to be the same size, within one degree or arc. Yet, the moon is much smaller than earth and only 238,900 miles away; yet the sun is massive, 99% of the mass of our solar system and 92.96 million miles away. So why do they look as if they are the same size? One can simply say it is the Deity's way of reminding us s/he set it up that way. Or perhaps it is a coincidence or a perfect occurrence. Miracles are in the eye of the beholder. One can witness an actual childbirth child and see it as miracle, or view it as nature (whatever that is) at work.

Miracle 8

But miracles occur in Israel almost everyday. The US with all of our military might, was unable to free our hostages out of Tehran in 1978. Yet, the highly successful counter-terrorist hostage rescue mission – Operation Entebbe – carried out in 1976 by the Israeli Defense Forces (whose military at that time was 100th the size of our military) can only be labeled a true miracle. This very tricky covert operation with numerous logistical challenges successfully freed over 90 hostages with minimal injuries and loss of life. One Israeli soldier was only milliseconds from death; yet only divine intervention could explain the following:

"... 'A fourth hijacker was hiding behind a pillar and pointed his gun to shoot at Amos [Goren]. And a fraction of a second before him, Amos shot him. "We checked his [the hijacker's] gun and he had already pulled the trigger - the piston had moved forwards through the cylinder, but Amos's bullet hit the cylinder and the bullet didn't lock and fire. Even the best director could not have planned it better', says Ofer..."[52]

Notably, the only IDF death during the 90-minute raid was the unit commander, the older brother of current Israeli Prime Minister Netanyahu.

Most of us have heard of Israel's Iron Dome, an air defense system that intercepts and destroys short-range rockets and artillery shells destined for populated areas. The Iron Dome is thought to be perfect; the Israeli government promotes it as invincible, but it is not. An Israeli Commander who is in charge of an Iron Dome Battery (which consists of a radar unit, missile control unit, and several launchers/interceptor missiles) reported the following:

Miracle 9

"A missile was fired from Gaza. The Iron Dome precisely calculated its trajectory but then failed to intercept the incoming rocket headed towards Tel Aviv. We know where these missiles are going to land to a radius of 200 meters. This particular missile was going to hit either the Azrieli Towers (Israel's equivalent of the pentagon) or a central Tel Aviv railroad station. Hundreds could have died. We fired the first (interceptor). It missed. Second interceptor; it missed. This is very rare. I was in shock. At this point, we had just four seconds until the missile landed. We already notified emergency services to converge on the target location, and warned of a mass casualty incident. Suddenly, the Iron Dome (which calculates wind speeds, among other things) showed a major wind coming from the east. That wind sent the missile into the sea! We were all stunned. I stood up and shouted, "There is a God!" "I witnessed this miracle with my own eyes. It was not told or reported to me. I saw the hand of God send that missile into the sea."[53]

Miracle 10

A bit further back in history, another miracle occurred during a battle in the Golan Heights between Syria and Israel in 1958 in which Syria had the upper hand. Israeli officer Gershon Salomon had the misfortune of being run over by an Israeli, snapping his spine. The Syrians ran over to shoot the wounded Israeli soldiers and take over the battlefield. As they were about to shoot Salomon, they dropped their weapons and ran away. Later, these same Syrian soldiers reported to the United Nations officers that they had seen thousands of angels surrounding the wounded Salomon, so they fled.[54]

VACATIONING WITH GOD

Miracle 11

A Reserve Tank Commander, Lt. Zwi Greengold, age 21, was in his kibbutz on Yom Kippur 1973 when he heard jet fighters overhead; realizing this meant serious trouble. He made his way north to the Golan Heights where Israeli forces were very much outnumbered. When he reached the Israeli Defense Force command center, he took command of two tanks and assembled two makeshift crews. Through sheer wit, determination and brilliant tactics, Greengold singlehandedly prevented two large Syrian contingents from breaking through Israeli lines. Many hours later, he returned back to the base and joined up with Israeli armored brigade; however they were in retreat as 80 Syrian tanks were just about take over the Command Center. Greengold fired upon the Syrian tanks that were on the verge of destroying an Israeli anti-tank unit inside the Command Center. The battle was almost lost, but somehow, the Israelis prevailed and pushed the Syrians out of the base. Greengold had been in battle for 20 hours nonstop despite being badly burned and had destroyed upwards of 30 Syrian tanks.[55][56]

Destroying more than 30 tanks in one battle lasting approximately 20 hours earned Greengold the title of Top Tank Commander in Modern History.[57]

In comparison, here are the statistics of two other top Tank "Ace" fighters in history:

The top recognized Tank Ace in history is Kurt Knispel (Germany, Blitskreig). He is officially credited with destroying 168 Allied tanks; some unconfirmed reports indicate the number might be as high as 195.[58]

These victories, however, occurred during many, many missions over the four-year period, 1941-1945.

The greatest lethal tank attack in history occurred during WWII in 1944. In this attack, German Captain, Michael Wittmann destroyed as many as 14 tanks, 2 antitank guns, and 15 other vehicles in a 15-hour time period against the British 7th Armored Division.[59]

What makes Greengold's accomplishment seem impossible was that the Israeli tanks, modified Centurions, were inferior to the later model, Russian supplied, T-62 tanks used by Syria. More remarkably, it is very important to note that the tanks the German Aces in WWII were extremely superior to those used by the Allies.

Miracle 12

Fighting in the Gaza Strip, 2014, Brigade commander Ofer Winter says a mysterious cloud shrouded his troops during attack. (Sounds familiar, doesn't it?) Winter claimed to have witnessed a miraculous occurrence, the likes of which he had never seen before during his military career.

He said that a predawn raid that was intended to make use of the dark as concealment was delayed, forcing the soldiers to move toward their objective as the sun was about to rise. The soldiers were in danger of being revealed in the light but, Winter recalled, a heavy fog descended to cover their movements until the objective was achieved.

"Suddenly a cloud protected us," he said, make a reference to the clouds that the Bible says protected the Israelites as they wandered in the desert. "Clouds of glory." Only when the soldiers were in a secure position did the fog dissipate, he said.

"It really was a fulfillment of the verse 'For the Lord your God is the one who goes with you to give you victory,'" he said, quoting a passage from Deuteronomy.[60]

Miracles still happen to this day. Go to Israel.

As I review this material, I again ask myself the question, "Why is the Israeli soil so holy?" I have found spiritual energy at other locations on the globe - an island near the North Pole, a mountain in the Australian Outback, a cave in Greece, a spot on the Ganges River. But, at least for me, the concentration of this type of energy is in Israel.

And then it came to me. Thinking again about the quotes about the Jews from some of the world's greatest thinkers, I surmised a connection. The force of humanity contains all people, with Christians, Jews and Muslims comprising the largest portion. And this energy of humankind started with a connection to the soil.

VACATIONING WITH GOD

As a group, the Western Religions are part of a colossal tree with a massive root system. The Hebrew connection to the Godhead occurs through those strong and indivisible roots. Thus, these three religions and a few other outliers (the Baha'i, Mormons, Puritans and Druids, are all attached to this holy root. Come kiss the sacred earth in which the holy root is buried: the land and soil of Israel.

"What a miracle life is and how alike are the souls when they send their roots down deep."
Nikos Kazantzakis

To people reading about history of wars and battles, they only see the visible universe. They can't comprehend the invisible hand of God.

I sat on a mound about 8 feet high. This is the place where a bunch of fighters who survived the Polish Ghetto, armed with only rifles and molotov cocktails, stopped a group of Egyptian tanks and soldiers with heavy weapons. What put fear in the Egyptians' hearts? (These battles occurred during the Revolutionary War in 1947.) The Israelis uses a handful of American pilots, using outdated, underpowered, fighter jets that were obtained from Czechoslovakia. They dropped several bombs on the main Egyptian tank force and the Egyptian General panicked and halted their advance. From my perspective, having sensed this fear, as I confronted my own subconscious, I understood the Deity was the one that put the fear into the Egyptian Officers and paralyzed them, which allowed the Israelis to win this impossible war! Miracles continue to happen in Israel throughout history because God commands the action.

David and Goliath

The most famous underdog story in history is the battle of David and Goliath, when a young shepherd, David, defeats Goliath, a heavily armed, giant warrior. Goliath wore armor that weighed 125 pounds, which included protection of his forehead and nose and it is said that his sword had marvelous powers. Archeologists know that the Philistines were using iron at that time. They would not give the Israelites information to learn how to make iron. Therefore, they had to use bronze, which is an inferior metal. During past battles, Goliath's armor fends off sword strikes and arrows. Yet a stone cast from a boy's slingshot broke the iron helmet, protecting Goliath's forehead and paralyzed this ferocious warrior! **"THIS IS SIMPLY IMPOSSIBLE!"** Another interesting fact of this battle is, instead of Goliath falling backward, from the momentum of the stone's hit, he fell forward. To me, the explanation is simple; the invisible hand of God delivered this deadly blow to the back of his head.

According to tradition, there are some facts that were too sacred be to put in written form, so they were passed verbally, from Priest to Priest. This story of David is told by Philo of Alexandria. Before David fights Goliath, Saul offers him his own armor. Saul speaks to him about the battle and David refuses the armor. He tells Saul, "I trust in God to fight the battle for me." David approaches Goliath, and hurls a stone at him, with a leather slingshot. Goliath is hit and falls forward on the ground.

After David strikes Goliath with the stone he runs to Goliath before he dies and Goliath says, "Hurry and kill me and rejoice." and David replies "Before you die, open your eyes and see your slayer." Goliath sees an angel and tells David that it is not he who has killed him but the angel, David agrees with him. Philo of Alexandria, then goes on to say that the angel of the Lord changes David's appearance so that no one recognizes him. Strangely, Saul did not recognize him as the person he knew before Goliath's death, and thus Saul asks Abner who he was.

1 Samuel 17, 57:45.

VACATIONING WITH GOD

NOTE:

We know from archeology, that the original warriors wore armor made of leather. Interesting enough, (this why Orthodox Jewish men put on Tfillan and pray twice a day). As metal was invented and swords were made of bronze, which could through leather, so they began to make armor out of the bronze as well. In turn, when iron was invented, helmets and armor were made of iron. We know the Philistines had iron and therefore we knew the heavy weight of Golith's armor was because it was made of iron.

Today, through the technology available, we can tell the velocity of a flying objects. From the data, we know that a rock flung from a leather slingshot is approximately 88 feet per second. The speed of a golf ball (hit by a Pro) is approximately 270 per second. We also know that the speed of a baseball thrown by a Pro is approximately 99 mph or 140 feet per second. From momentum calculation from the strike of an iron sword would destroy a warrior wearing armor of leather and bronze. Many of us have seen a batter get hit by a baseball, while watching a game. The energy of a baseball, when pitched, is two times the energy of a rock that is slung. When the batter is hit by a ball, he generally does not fall down, unless he is hit in the head. Baseball players are protected from this event because they wear helmets made from heavy plastic. We have all seen the baseball bounce off the helmet without harming the batter. The players do not wear iron helmets because they weigh too much for their heads. Therefore, we realize, that a stone flung from a slingshot could not harm someone wearing a baseball or iron helmet.

We now understand David's comment, "I trust in God to fight the battle for me." God's angel protects him.

Today, after the many miraculous victories of Israeli battles, such as the War of Independence, 6-Day War, the Raid on Entebbe, many Israelis still do not believe that God has won these battles for them. They have forgotten David's words, "On this day, Hashem will deliver you into my hands. I shall smite you… Then the whole world will know there is a God in Israel. And this Assembly will know that not through sword and spear, does Hashem grant salvation. For unto Hashem is the battle and he shall deliver you into our hands." 1 Samuel 17:47 We now can understand, the various Israeli soldiers who have seen angels battle for them, just as David did.

Note:

God's name was considered a very serious and powerful thing, so much so that one of the Ten Commandments prohibits us from saying God's name in vain. As a result, people have come up with various substitutions. God is often referred to as Hashem, which translated, means "The Name", as a creative way of not saying God's name.

The British had defeated the French in the French and Indian Wars. Knowing this fact, when you think about the American Revolutionary War, why would the British lose the war to a weak, ill-trained Continental Army? This army was an ill-equipped, ill-provisioned, impoverished, underpaid, vagabond army. I believe God also won this war for the Americans. I contend, that when Israel fights a sacred battle, one that protects the Holy Land; God (Hashem) has and will continue to fight the battle for them. Just as he did when George Washington, with his inadequate forces defeated the mighty British.

GOD BLESS AMERICA! GOD BLESS ISRAEL!

CHAPTER TWELVE
PART B
MIRACLES

MAN TOUCHING GOD - THE PAST
The history, birth and development of Israel is well-known, and I do not need to repeat it in this book. However, I have different "glasses" than other historians and writers. I see the world through God's covered lenses, so my story will be a little different than the others'.

It is interesting to note, that the history of Israel, just like in the time of the American Revolution, in American History... Here are some great humans in Israeli history and today: Theodor Herzl, Chaim Weizmann, David Ben Gurion, Moshe Dayan, Golda Meir, Yitzhak Rabin, Binyamin Netanyahu, Shimon Peres and Ehud Barak, Elie Wiesel.

Interestingly enough, the modern State of Israel starts in France, with the Dreyfus Affair. The scandal began in 1894, with the treason conviction of Captain Alfred Dreyfus, a young Jewish, French artillery officer sentenced to life imprisonment for allegedly communicating French military secrets to the German Embassy in Paris, Dreyfus was imprisoned on Devil's Island in French Guiana, where he spent nearly five years.

In 1896, a French Army Major named Ferdinand Walsin Esterházy, was identified as the real culprit. After anti-Semitic, high-ranking military officials covered up the evidence, a military court acquitted Esterházy after a trial lasting only two days. The Army then accused Dreyfus with additional charges based on falsified documents.

A Jewish man named Theodor Herzl, was a playwright and a journalist from the Viennese newspaper, Neue Freie Presse, covering the action. He witnessed crowds in the streets, screaming, "Kill the Jews!". Naturally, this was extremely disturbing to him.

Before we discuss Herzl further, let's first discuss the effects this scandal had on France. As much as we have seen the effect of Jews on America, the great French writers, which were lead by Emile Zola, a major figure in the political liberalization of France and in the exoneration of the falsely accused and convicted army officer Alfred Dreyfus. They came to the aid of Dreyfus and he was finally released from prison. Through the injustice and unfair treatment they witnessed, the people of France and it's government realized there must be more freedom. Therefore, France adopted the American way of separation of Church and State. So, as you can see, a situation that started out as anti-Semitic and negative turned into the blossoming of France, which caught them up in many ways to America.

Let's now discuss Theodor Herzl. Herzl was a tall handsome man and had olive-toned skin. He was a secular, and did not see his Jewish religion as a benefit, but saw it as a negative. He did not like his dark olive features and wished he had fair skin, blonde hair and blue eyes.

Though he died long before its establishment, he is generally considered a father of the State of Israel, formed in 1948. Herzl is buried in Israel and next to him is a picture of an Iranian God that looks amazing identical to him. You may be wondering why God chose this individual to become a Prophet and change history. He was key in establishing and creating the energy that would be known today as Zionism.

VACATIONING WITH GOD

"I believe that a wondrous generation of Jews will spring into existence. The Maccabees will rise again. Let me repeat once more my opening words: The Jews who wish for a State will have it. We shall live at last as free men on our own soil, and die peacefully in our own homes. The world will be freed by our liberty, enriched by our wealth, magnified by our greatness. And whatever we attempt there to accomplish for our own welfare, will react powerfully and beneficially for the good of humanity."
- Theodore Herzl, concluding words of his book, The Jewish State.

NOTE:

God choosing Herzl is as unlikely as God choosing Moses. Freud wrote a book that I found interesting. He wrote that he believed that Moses was not Jewish, but was a Priest of Egypt under the rule of Pharaoh Akhenaten, and was cast out when the Pharaoh died. Freud believed that Moses could not speak Hebrew and that is why he stuttered and Aaron had to speak for him, but he was well-known in the Egyptian court. Moses became the Messenger of God and a Prophet.

We return to Herzl, this strange, tall, dark, man being converted by what he saw in the Dreyfus Affair and is burning with desire to create a Jewish state. He puts all his energy into the creation of Zionism. He returned home, to Vienna and had a mental breakdown for two weeks. Everything in him had completely changed.

"I think for me, life has ended and world history has begun... At night it burns within me when my eyes are closed; I cannot hide from it."
-Theodor Herzl

From my view as a Jungian, (a believer in Carl Jung's teachings), his collective unconscious had taken over his wheelhouse. The collective unconscious, not his ego, was now in control of his life. (* See note) Perhaps only other Jungians will understand this transformation. Carl Jung discusses this in great detail and the dreams of his periods of craziness in his Red Book.

The author of The Last Temptation of Christ, Nikos Kazantzakis also writes in his memo to Greco… "There are two parts to my consciousness, the human/ego consciousness and the consciousness of the Deity. They both wrestle for control over my behavior and actions." I believe this is what happened to Herzl. His ego state was completely turned over and his collective subconscious, (the God part of him) controlled his actions and behaviors. He became God's messenger and servant totally dedicated to the cause of creating the state of Israel. He was willing to sacrifice his mortal body to achieve this goal. Was Herzl a Prophet? In the times of the Old Testament, many people said that God had spoken to them, so how would the population know if they actually did? They waited for the test of time to see if their predictions came true. Herzl predicted that the State of Israel would be born in 50 years (well after his death) and he was correct.

Ziontist Start

The first Zionist Congress was held in Basel, Switzerland, in 1897 at which the World Zionist Organization was founded and Herzl was elected president. In 1902 Herzl published his utopian vision of the Jewish state, the *Altneuland* ("Old New Land"). Herzl was becoming frustrated with the lack of progress, and realized that anti-Semitism would never go away. At the Fifth Zionist Congress, he delivered a passionate plea for a fund to be created to help establish the Jewish State. His speech turned the delegates around, the motion passed and the congress resolved that a fund to be called ***Jewish National Fund*** should be established, and that "the fund shall be the property of the Jewish people as a whole." ***JNF***'s first undertaking was the collection of £200,000. One of the delegates immediately pledged £10. Herzl made the second donation and his aide, the third. And with this, the dream of a national fund that was used to build the foundations of a Jewish state became a reality. Very soon after, it was proposed that a collection box be placed in every Jewish home so that contributions could be made to JNF at every opportunity. In the period between the two World Wars, about one million Blue Boxes could be found in Jewish homes throughout the world.

VACATIONING WITH GOD

Herzl had considered other locations for the Jewish Holy Land. The British considered land in Africa, but the Russian Jews that were moving to Israel, demanded that they chose the Holy Land of Israel.

It is interesting to note that another non-Jew understood this phenomenon;

"A Rabbi was once asked the following question: 'When you say that the Jews should return to Palestine, you mean, surely, the heavenly, the immaterial, the spiritual Palestine, our true homeland?' The Rabbi jabbed his staff into the ground in wrath and shouted, 'No! I want Palestine down here, the one you can touch with your hands, with its stones, its thorns and its mud!'"
-Nikos Kazantzakis

Jewish National Fund

In the spring of 1903 JNF purchased its first parcel of land: 50 acres in Hadera with funds given as a gift by the well-known philanthropist Isaac (Yitzhak Leib) Goldberg. In 1904, JNF was called upon to carry out its first mission, financing the expenses of Jewish scientists, which was the start of JNF's work in research and development. By 1905, JNF land holdings had expanded to include land near the Sea of Galilee, and at Ben Shemen in the center of the country. Then they bought an area in the center of the country at Hulda. The land at Hulda was bought for a very special purpose -- the planting of olive groves in memory of Herzl -- and with this, JNF embarked on a new venture: changing the land from desert to forest. A major effort has been started and continues to this day to plant trees in Israel. Much of the brown, barren land is now trees, forest, parks and completely green.

In this first decade of its existence, land acquisition was not JNF's only focus. The Jewish National Fund also played an important role in establishing the first modern Jewish city, Tel Aviv.

The JNF created the first collective community (known today as kibbutzim). Kibbutzim are such a large part of Israel, today. JNF also set up and administered farms; continuing its programs of creating and maintaining new forest areas, to this day, which is so important to the development of Israel.

For many years, JNF has been working to build Israel's water economy by developing alternative water sources, saving the economy millions, advancing Israeli agriculture, and improving water quality. JNF's work with water includes the treatment, recycling, and collection of both waste and runoff water, responsible aquifer drilling, and river rehabilitation. Over the past three decades JNF has helped build over 250 reservoirs, which has raised the amount of recycled water in Israel from 4% to over 85% today. Furthermore, over half of Israel's agricultural water comes from recycled and reused wastewater, and most of that water is supplied by JNF reservoirs.

Taking a child to school, driving to the office, going to the market - all activities we all take for granted. Along Israel's northern border however, these every day acts mean risking exposure to sniper gunfire. JNF has constructed security roads out of view of the Lebanese border. Shielding travelers from those who would do them harm, therefore, allowing them to live and participate in normal every-day activities without harm.

"Operation Security Blanket" is a program that Jewish National Fund has created in response to the ongoing rocket attacks that have plagued southern Israel. It is an emergency campaign empowering American Jews to provide immediate relief for Israeli children and their families living in areas under rocket attack along the Gaza border.

The Israel Defense Force is among the most courageous and most disciplined in the world. Young Israeli men and women serve up to three years of mandatory military service. Their heroic determination to protect the Holy Land and the children of Israel is legendary. But these soldiers are merely children themselves. And unlike Americans, whose first experience away from home is often the joy of going to college, Israel high school graduates enter the army – service, fraught with loneliness and fear. That is why JNF creates comfortable facilities where these worthy young heroes can gather with family and friends on those

VACATIONING WITH GOD

precious occasions when they can meet and enjoy pleasant moments with loved ones while serving their country.

JNF battles approximately 1,000 forest fires every year during the five fire-prone months. Half of these are caused by arson and hostile actions. With a commitment to research, equipment and training, JNF is making huge progress in minimizing loss. After 10,000 acres of hand-planted forest were destroyed by Katyusha rockets in the summer of 2006, JNF launched Operation Northern Renewal to help replant and replace the topsoil that was burned away. JNF also replaced Israel's aging fleet of fire trucks with new, compact trucks that can more easily maneuver in forests or city streets.

JNF is instrumental in founding secondary schools and pioneering higher education as well.

From its beginning, as an initial part of the Zionist Movement, to current time, where it is an integral part of the Israeli Culture.

In summary, I believe, that without the JNF, Israel would not be the strong country it is today.

NOTE:

In order to understand this book, I must try to explain something that is unexplainable, complex and difficult to present; It is the theory of Carl Jung. The only way to explain the miraculous events of the American Revolution and Israel's birth, is to try to understand the Collective unconscious, which Jung explained first in 1912. Jung's mentor was Sigmund Freud, the father of Psychology. Freud had brought forth the concept that the character that we present to the world, our personal identity, is a conscious force which he called the ego. He then explained that below this conscious force was a psychological activity that contained all of the history of the individual in his unconsciousness. A child under hypnosis can describe what his/her crib looked like at the age of 6 months. None of this is available to the ego. Freud explained that negative experiences to the child are recorded as well and forgotten.

This is called infant amnesia. Furthermore, these repressed memories affect the individual's behavior. When a young child is molested/raped by an older family member, this can scar them for life. They must deal with a continuous battle as an adult, and must do continuous work to overcome the damage done by this horrific experience of their past. Jung added another level to Freud's theory... He stated below the first unconscious was the Collective unconscious. We have touched upon this in the discussion about the participation mystique. The Collective unconscious contains all of the consciousness of our species. In animals, we call this, an instinct. Simple creatures are not to be taught anything by their parents, but the memory of the species survival is their consciousness and they react to their environment in a prescribed manner. Human beings and other mammals have the same collective memory, but are also taught by their parents. We believe humans have the largest ego of all creatures on the planet. There is a Jewish collective, just as there is a Christian collective and Muslim collective. All of these are of the same level within the psyche – the human collective. "You are a people consecrates Yod-Hey-Vav-Hey, your God and Yod-Hey-Vav-Hey has chosen you to be His very own people out of all of the peoples of the Earth" Deuteronomy 14:2.

The last adventure in this book is not a spiritual one, but is deeply emotional. (It happened after my final draft of the book, but I have decided to include it.)

A friend of mine, who works for JNF, recently took his family to Israel. They visited many of the JNF facilities that I have mentioned earlier. As part of their travels, they visited Aleh Negev, a special healing center where the JNF provides care for young adults with multiple disabilities. He told me the following, "The moment that my family realized the importance of JNF is when we visited Aleh Negev! While we were at Aleh Negev, we met a family that was visiting with their 21 year old, wheel-chair bound son, who should not have survived past the age of 10. When our guide introduced me as the Executive Director of JNF, Los Angeles, the family could not thank me enough for the work we do. They said, "We could not live a normal life without JNF, toda raba (Hebrew for gratitude and deepest thanks) from the bottom of our hearts!" I was crying; my wife was crying; my daughters were crying. On the ride back to Tel Aviv, my family told me how proud they were of me and the work JNF is doing on behalf of the people of Israel." Perhaps I am wrong, but to me, this exchange was both an emotional and spiritual experience, as Herzl's spirit and the Deity were crying with them. These moments are holy, as human consciousness becomes a microcosm of the macrocosm that ties Humanity to the Deity and the Deity to Humanity.

The Jewish people have become God's Priests and this explains their miraculous existence. As the Collective Carrier of the Deity's symbolism and desires, the Jewish people and the state of Israel are indestructible.

I believe Israel and the United States will continue to flourish and grow and become the seed bed for the coming of the Messiah, as long as a significant portion of their people continue to believe in and love God. This powerful love gives them the power and force to love one another.

CHAPTER TWELVE
PART C

12 - PART C - THE FUTURE

This whmiraculous fact that both the United States and Israel should not have been created and have survived to this day, and have become more powerful? When we look back at the history of civilization, specifically, western culture and western science, it is a true miracle that the United States was created. When this happened it totally changed the method, economy and belief systems of the people in the world. Another miracle is the fact, that today, the Jewish Homeland of Israel is back, and provides a place for Jews to live and is run by the Jewish Leaders.

So what is the future? If we believe in our Deity; if we maintain our religions and do not become secular and materialistic, they will continue to exist. However, if we discontinue our moral and ethical values and our belief in religions and spirituality, we will lose our Deity's love and will fade away like the other civilizations have, as Toynbee wrote about."

Today, there are several non-profit organizations that support Israel and the Zionistic movement in Israel, the United States and Europe. There are organizations that offer sponsored trips for American and European teens and young adults to visit Israel. Some organizations collect money to plant and grow trees in Israel and help with agricultural growth. Other are investing in technology that has/is based out of Israel.

The Jewish National Fund is still one of the most valuable contributors to our Holy Land. JNF continues to make a difference for generations to come. They do this by continuing to build communities, work with forestry and green innovations, research and development, education and more, in Israel.

They are also in the United States and Europe, and focus on the importance of education and advocacy to schools and synagogues located in both the United States and Europe, to continue to support the Zionist Movement. There are many other Jewish and Christian organizations that continue to help the immigration of Jews from other countries to this day.

"When I was younger, I wanted to change the world. Now wiser, I want to change myself."
-Rumi

NOTE:

To me the Author: the simple fact you have read this spiritual book is a minor miracle… G_D BLESS.

AFTERWORD
TRAVELING AS A PILGRIM

The object of this book was to induce and seduce you to travel to Israel, not just to visit the historical sites of a dynamic, growing country as a tourist, but to also try to get in touch with your own soul. Allow me to explain why I am so bold in my thinking to make this statement.

When we were a primitive people, we lived directly on mother earth and were able to understand its subtle vibrations. We had a relationship with the local patterns of energy and we assumed these strong forces were "Gods."

Additionally, we had a relationship with our inner spirit/life force energy or life breath, called *Chi* in Chinese medicine. The Hebrew word *Ruach* means wind, breath or spirit and refers to the same concept. This inner life energy allowed us to have a direct relationship filled with love and reverence to mother earth (e.g. nature). We honored the spirit that existed in all living things; for example, after killing animals for food, we tasted it's blood, honored it and thanked it for its sacrifice.

Due to our vast agricultural, industrial, engineering and scientific advances over multiple millennia, we have lost these relationships to nature, and even to our own inner beings. Plus, it is difficult for humans today to sense faint energy sources as very large manmade electronic fields and vibrations bombard our planet. It appears as if mankind's sole objective is the systematic pursuit of smarter gadgets, virtual realities and artificial intelligence.

However, we must find a way back to our fundamental understanding of the world through connections with Mother Earth. This is vital to our very existence - or else we run the risk of destroying our own environment. We need to reconnect with that "still, small voice" within nature and ourselves by feeling the trees and the grass, by sitting quietly on the mountain tops and the edge of the sea, and listen to the silence. Additionally, we must devise solutions to reuse the materials of our technological world to make them harmonious with nature.

Typically, the route to become one again with Mother Nature is found by a deep religious quest, by delving deeply into prayer or by Buddhist meditation. But these paths are difficult to follow in today's world.

Traveling to Israel allows us the opportunity to experience our historical religious figures - be they Christ, Moses, Mohamed, The Virgin Mary or King David - as their energy vibrations are still present in the Holy Land, alive and ready to be absorbed. Our ancient ancestors were completely in touch with their inner life force, and as such, their God-nature as well as their Human-nature. When you literally breathe the same noble gasses as all our primal forefathers, you can open up yourself to the mystery and the majesty of God. By choosing this voyage, you also partake in man's great journey to become enlightened.

If you still need convincing to visit Israel, the following is a spiritual reason based upon evolution. Until recently, it was believed that Neanderthals were not capable of speech. But in 1989, a hyoid bone[61] was discovered, not in East Africa as might be expected, but in the Kebara cave located in northern Israel. Why is this significant? Since it was in the land of Israel that God first communicated with Man, we might infer that in order for the Deity's wishes to be communicated to all, humans needed the ability to speak to one another.

This book was *not* written for Israelis; they already live in the middle of the hand of God, working that holy soil and eating its produce. Think of Israel as the merger of God and Man – where humans can step upwards and internalize the divine spark of God, allowing us to become aware of our inner, and perhaps better, selves. Thus, this book is for Americans and Canadians who wish to expand their mind, body and soul beyond the materialistic society in which we live. This is especially true for young Christians and Jews to touch their HOMELAND, the land that birthed their religion and moral beliefs.

If you are a Christian, perhaps like Constantine and Pascal, you may see a cross in the sky or feel its emanations. If you are Jewish, you may sense your people's history as an integrated whole. If you are a Muslim, you must visit Haifa, for there you will find that the Israeli Arabs and the Jews live in peace and harmony, and Muslims are as well integrated into the population as they are in the US. These Israeli Arabs enjoy one of the highest standards of living in the Middle East, and make up a large percentage of the students at the University of Haifa.

The energies in Israel will give you the understanding that we are all brothers and sisters, all of one race, the race of humankind. And the goal of this race? To bring the greatness and glory of God into this world, as individuals, and as collective. Going to Israel

At the beginning of this book, I suggested that people travel to Israel to get in touch with their spiritual self. In particular, I advocate that young adults/late teens spend several months in Israel - either on an Israeli kibbutz, volunteering for a nonprofit organization or taking classes at a University - in order to experience a very different reality than what one is accustomed to in America. This is especially true for Jewish youth to find their identity amongst their brethren. While many Jewish American parents choose to have their child's Bar/Bat Mitzvah in Jerusalem, I believe 13 year olds will not receive the same benefits as older youth; they are still under their parents' control and may not be capable of being away from their parents for extended time period.

It is vital that adults visit Israel to communicate with their God. For Jewish individuals, the regular tourist loop should include Hebron and Beersheba. When you get off the tour bus, try to internalize the sights, sounds, and smells, but mostly, interact with Israeli residents. Research the various American/Israeli tours and choose one that will offer you the opportunity to mingle with the local population. Otherwise, your interactions with Israeli residents will be limited to tour guides and those who work in hotels and food service.

Be aware that the sites you will visit, especially in Jerusalem, are a part of the Old Testament; thus, the Deity lives within them. This will assist you to understand yourself in relation to the Deity, the Jewish collective and to the collective of the entire world.

I believe Christian adults should make a similar journey and visit Bethlehem, Nazareth and Tiberias, which is located next to the Sea of Galilee/Lake Kineret. In particular, visit the ancient city of Capernaum – it is believed to be Christ's home and the center of his ministry after he left Nazareth. You will want to see the ancient synagogue where Jesus held regular sermons. You might wish to meditate at these sites; the energy of Christ and his message can be felt. It will help you to understand your relationship to the community of Christians and to the world's collective.

The Western World knows the monotheistic God, but has lost its relationship with nature. While primitive people did not have a monotheistic God, they lived with their Gods and were part of natural world.

An enlightened individual can be in touch with both worlds if s/he is open to them. One must find the proper place, the proper door and the proper key. I am suggesting the proper place is Israel. The proper door is the your religious past intermingling with the energies of these

VACATIONING WITH GOD

extraordinary historical sights. Lastly, the proper key is prayer and meditation in the Lord's House (eg Israel).

The connection between Judaism, Christianity and Islam is that unique individual souls can touch the Godhead, and it is the belief that Jesus was a man who also received "Christ-consciousness."[62] However, that terminology might cause a negative reaction from both Muslims and Jews; while Christ was never a Christian, his name has become synonymous with Christianity. A more acceptable term would be God-consciousness. The three major religions share the similar belief in a monotheistic Deity, whereby Moses, Christ and Muhammad are enlightened after being touched by the God-source.

God-consciousness should be the unifying principle between all peoples. Historical prophets were not the only ones touched by the source; people of modern times – Gandhi; Mother Theresa; Martin Luther King; Nelson Mandela – have also been touched by this force. Plato's teachings reflect this wisdom, and the Sufis[63] live in this knowledge. Others touched by this force include the great poets, such as Rumi, Wadsworth, Whitman and Keats, gurus in India, Buddha and Lao Tse.

This force is very much alive, and is available to anyone who wishes to dive deeply into him or herself. I have traveled the world over, and the location where it can be most easily assessed is the State of Israel.

The entire object of this book was openly to seduce you; to ask you; to invite you; to pray to you; to meet yourself. Your own unique, special soul. By visiting, touching, seeing, feeling, hearing and smelling the Holy land/soil of Israel, you have a chance of accomplishing this goal. When you are in Israel, any time you eat the food, whether it be grains, vegetables or meat raised or grown in the Holy land, you are ingesting a part of Israel into yourself. The energy of Israel may be the ecstatic force/numinous experiences which may help unlock the inner pathway to yourself.

Thomas Moore, who I quoted earlier in this book has written two marvelous books: Care of the Soul and The Re-enchantment of Everyday Life. His argument and mine, is that, to survive in this materialistic world, we must work hard to see the invisible and find the magical pathway through the wall that surrounds us. Our ego is too strong and holds the sword that protects us. We, like David, must learn to control this force, instead of it controlling us. Hopefully the material in this book will give you a light through the darkness.

If you are aware of one or many ecstatic forces/numinous experiences in the past, Israel may give you many more and the possible explanation to the deep meaning of these Holy experiences.

I hope when you read (and re-read this book), it can open up the celestial rhythms; the hologram of the Micro and Macro of the universe. This awareness give us more ability to touch our souls and the soul (Deity) of the universe. This will make us understand that we are blessed and live in love and blessings. You come to understand, each one of us is like a grain of sand on an enormous beach. As such we are part of the energy of the whole beach (perhaps a better simile would be you are a drop of water in the oceans of the world and yet contain within you at the most microscopic level, all the elements of the entire ocean). You are affected by the energy of the whole beach/ocean, you also affect it and are a great force in its transformation. For the grains/drops touching you can change as you have changed. They in turn, can change those grains/drops around them in the most positive way. This can then help change the world we live in.

You dance with the Sufis, you radiate light and distribute positive energy to all that you meet.

Someday after mastering the winds, the waves, the tides and gravity, we shall harness... the energies of love, and then for a second time in the history of the world, man will discover fire.
-Pierre Teilhard de Chardin

APPENDIX

One would think that the majority of the people and tour groups that visit Israel are Jewish. The fact is, more Christians visit Israel each year than Jews, from North America. Similar to the well-know Birthright Tour (for Jewish young adults), there is a program for college students called Covenant Israel. It was founded by Matt Stover in 2011. A Covenant Journey tour of Israel is designed specifically to motivate college students to discover and affirm their Christian faith and identity through an experiential journey and educational experience of Biblical, historic, and modern Israel, equipping them to be goodwill ambassadors for Israel; giving the participants the ability to advocate for Israel upon their return home. There are many other tours offered to people of all ages that the main focus is on the Christian faith.

The greatest gift that is offered to Jewish young adults (ages 18-26) from the United States and Canada, is a trip called Birthright Israel. Founded in 1999 by a remarkable group of committed Jewish philanthropists led by Charles Bronfman and Michael Steinhardt, Birthright Israel aims to strengthen Jewish identity, Jewish communities, and connection with Israel and its people. Birthright Israel works with accredited tour groups to provide the gift of a free 10-day trip to Israel. Birthright Israel coordinates all air travel, sets up high educational and quality trips for these young adults.

The JNF contributes to the Birthright programs and offers several different missions and tours, as well. With access to many sites and places that most tourists are not allowed to visit, participants are guaranteed a unique experience and gain a new perspective on Israel. On some tours, JNF has some same-age IDF soldiers join the tour, which makes for a unique and very rewarding experience for all.

They have tours geared towards different age groups and interests. Some examples of their tours are; a tour for young professionals ages 30-45; a tour for adults 55 and older; a culinary, wine and music tour, and many more.

"Inspire a woman, you inspire a family. Inspire enough families, you inspire a community. Inspire enough communities, you can change the world." This is the key quote of the Jewish Women's Renaissance Program. Founded in 2008. This program is designed for mothers who have children under the age of 18 living at home. They have also started a program for dads. The eight-day journey is designed to give mom and dads a deep, eternal connection to Israel, a profound kinship with each other, and a heart filled with Jewish values.

A couple other concepts that are geared for Interfaith groups also offer a great opportunity to experience the Holy Land. One is a program called Honeymoon Israel. Their vision is that every committed couple with at least one Jewish partner will possess the basic knowledge, inspiration, support system, and sense of belonging to build a family with meaningful connections to Jewish life and the Jewish people, thereby enhancing and strengthening the Jewish community. Although this program is not completely free, it is highly subsidized.

Another program is Israel Teen Fellowship. Israel Teen Fellowship is a two-week journey throughout Israel that focuses on diversity and welcomes teenagers of all Faiths, in 9th-12th grade. Participants meet and interact with members of various communities, including: Jews, Arabs, Bedouins, Druze, and LGBT. They also complete projects to help improve the communities they visit. This program was founded by Michael Dorfman.

In most cases, these sponsored trips are free, highly subsidized or scholarships/grants are available. When you are ready to take your journey to Israel, I recommend you research one of these tour programs and read the Bible. Reading the books written by the authors I have quoted, would be a benefit to you. These would help open the Pathways to yourself before and when you visit Israel.

SOMETIMES YOU HAVE TO GO FAR TO FIND YOURSELF!

ENDNOTES

1. http://www.poetrychaikhana.com/Poets/A/AttarFaridud/Lookingforyo/index.html
2. *Helena is vital figure in the history of Christianity, ensuring its place within Western Civilization. Not only did she determine Jesus' birthplace and site of his crucifixion, but she also had great influence over her son, Constantine the Great, who became a huge advocate of the religion. Emperor Constantine greatly endorsed Christianity in the Roman Empire. As the story goes, while about to engage in the Battle of the Milvian Bridge in 312 CE, he had a vision: he looked up to the sun and saw a cross of light above it, with the Greek words "in this sign, conquer!" After his victory, Constantine scaled back his participation in the traditional religions of Rome and becomes a patron to one particular branch of Christianity. Unfortunately, after becoming Emperor, he started persecuting Christians of other sects. The fact that Constantine viewed a cross and the Greek words in sky, and then is victorious, is considered by many to be a miracle. As an aside, it should be noted that approximately 275 years before Constantine, Saul (aka: Paul the Apostle), a Jew, became the greatest advocate of Jesus on the road to Damascus. Looking back now from our vantage point, we can see how these two events affected western civilization and indeed created the most populous religion of today, Christianity. The acceptance of Christianity in the Roman Empire was pivotal in history. At that time, the various Jewish sects had an ongoing internal debate about Jesus: was he simply a prophet, or the Son of God. After Rome embraced Christianity, many of the Jewish Romans became*

Christians. Additionally, before Constantine died, he came to Israel and built the Church of the Nativity.
3. *The purchase of the Cave of the Patriarchs (or Cave of the Machpelah) by Abraham from the Hittites some 3700 years ago established the Jews' attachment to land of Israel. The purchase of the cave with an adjoining field, and by Abraham settling in the area, literally lays the foundation of the first real estate of Israel, long before Joshua's conquest. Additionally, Abraham's agreement with/purchase from two local Amorite clans designates these Hittites as masters of the covenant. The patriarchs and matriarch of Israel - Abraham, Isaac, Jacob, Sarah, Rebecca and Leah - are all buried in this cave. (Missing is Rachel, who is buried near Bethlehem where she died during childbirth.)*
4. *Rachel's tomb is located on the northern edge of Bethlehem; she died during childbirth and Jacob buried her there. He placed a pillar on top of her grave, and Genesis 35:19-20 states it is there until this day. Since the beginning of the Byzantine Period (324-638 C.E.), pilgrims and travelers have described the tomb structure which has taken many forms throughout the years. In 1841, with a permit from the Turkish Sultan, Sir Moses Montefiore refurbished and expanded the tomb into the structure that stands today with its famous dome.*
5. *Otto (1869-1937) was an eminent German theologian and scholar of comparative religion*
6. *Eliade (1907-1986) was a Romanian historian of religion, philosopher and professor.*
7. *James (1842 - 1910) was an American philosopher and psychologist. He is not only known as the as the "Father of American Psychology" but is also believed by many to be one of the most to be one of the most influential philosophers in the US.*
8. *http://www.evelynunderhill.org/her_work/about_her_life.shtml*
9. *Weiner, Eric, (2011) Man Seeks God. New York, NY: Hachette Book Group (p. 32)*
10. *Cayce (1877-1945) had the ability to place himself in a semi trance in which he would lose consciousness. He called this experience a "transpersonal reality." He provided psychic readings within his trance state, mostly focused upon people's ailments and cures. Later in life, he focused on spiritual teachings, and from within his altered states,*

gave readings and lessons on dreams, developing intuition, karma, coincidence (synchronicity) and past life relationships.
11. Many years later I realized by behavior may have been caused by my own father/son relationship.
12. The earth itself has power, and an example closer to us in time and geography is the Native American sweat lodge. If you want to feel the tremendous power of Mother Nature, go through a sweat lodge experience.
13. Stonehenge, Machu Picchu and the Ayers Rock (Australia) are places that are significant in this regard, and the people who live in these regions are consciously aware of this importance.
14. http://www.whirling-dervish.org/history.htm
15. Israel is a small country, approximately the size of New Jersey. Located in the Middle East, it's bordered by the Mediterranean Sea on the west and the Gulf of Aqaba on the south; Egypt to the southwest; Jordan to the east; Syria to the northeast; and Lebanon to the north.
16. The location of the Foundation Stone is the holiest site in Judaism. It is viewed as the spiritual junction between Heaven and Earth as it was from this rock that the world was created, with the rock itself being the first part of the earth to come into existence. It was at this site that God gathered the earth that formed into Adam, and it was upon this rock that many of the early biblical figures offered sacrifices to God.
17. Despite being Jewish, I've had many experiences sensing the power of Mary and have met her in Guadalupe, Marmolada, Fatima, Sicily, Toronto, Lyon and Ephesus. Many Catholics would cherish some of these experiences; a priest with whom I discussed them asked for my permission to repeat these stories. Whenever called upon to do healing, I attempt to use Mary as one of my sources of energy. To me, she represents much more than Mary, mother of Christ - she symbolizes the great earth mother, the female power given to us from the womb. Over the last several hundred years in various locations around the world, groups of local children report meeting Mary. They consistently report an identical story: Mary tells them if only all of the people in the world would simultaneously pray for peace for only 5-6 minutes, we humans would achieve peace. You don't have to be Catholic to understand the power of this vision. Mary represents the earth mother ("represents" is not a strong enough term; she is the projection into

our reality of the earth mother). It is not imagination or illusion; the children do not suffer from hallucinations. For Jews, Mary is the Shekinah, (female version of God). At Guadalupe, Mexico, there is a church for this Mary projection to local children. A fabric showing a picture of Mary is placed upon the spot where the earlier aborigine people had a temple for worshipping the earth mother.

18. Despite my around-the-world travels, I saw faces only one time before, within the rocks and the trees at the Delphi in Greece. Far smaller in size, I believed the faces were guarding the Delphi. But on Mount Sinai, I felt them to be trapped forever. Or perhaps until the Messiah comes.

19. Examples: the Rosetta Stone; the figurines of the Gods from the Pantheon; a superior and more complete exhibit of Egyptian Sarcophagus than in the Cairo museum.

20. The Biblical Name for God.

21. Hillel lived 100 years before Christ (110BCE - 10 CE) and was a Judaic scholar, sage and Rabbi

22. http://jewishencyclopedia.com/articles/7698-hillel

23. "Young Nepalese Boy Slain in Human Sacrifice Ritual" http://www.cnn.com/2015/07/27/asia/nepal-human-sacrifice/

24. In his book, *Fear and Trembling*, Danish philosopher Kierkegaard (1813-1855) discusses the anxiety Abraham felt over God's request to sacrifice his adult son. Abraham resigned himself to the deed due to his deep belief in God; but his decision was *not* because he felt he must obey a God who was always right. Rather, he was willing to act unethically because he had faith that his God wouldn't do something that was ethically wrong (insist the sacrifice be carried forth). `http://www.sparknotes.com/philosophy/kierkegaard/section2.rhtml

25. When powerful Kings (e.g. Pharaohs) died, humans and animals were sacrificed with him. Today, we still follow this tradition of sacrificing a living entity upon death with flowers. Voluminous amounts of wreaths and flowers indicate the person's importance or the particular tragedy of his/her death.

26. In Genesis 9, the Noahic Covenant is God's promise to Noah to never again send a worldwide flood to destroy the earth as an act of divine judgment for man's sins. As a sign of that promise, the Deity placed a rainbow in the sky whenever it rained.

27. An ancient Indian text that became an important work of Hindu tradition within philosophy and literature
28. https://www.templeinstitute.org/red_heifer/red_heifer_contents.htm
29. http://itic.iocunesco.org/index.php?option=com_contentandview=articleandid=1133andItemid=2155
30. https://crete.wordpress.com/2009/11/05/killer-tsunamis-from-an-ancient-eruption/
31. Baruch Spinoza (1632-1677) was a Dutch philosopher of Jewish descent whose writings laid the foundations of the Enlightenment.
32. Ancient Jewish tradition of mystical interpretation of the Bible
33. "The Last 2 Million Years" http://www.aish.com/h/iid/48964091.html
34. In addition to being a philosopher, Pascal was a mathematician and scientist.
35. http://www.nytimes.com/1989/09/26/nyregion/dalai-lama-meets-jews-from-4-major-branches.html After the Assyrian Empire conquered the territories of central and northern Israel - known as the Kingdom of Israel - in 721 BCE, they took the Jews into captivity and expelled them to other regions of that empire.
36. Mark Twain, "Concerning The Jews," Harper's New Monthly Magazine 99 (September 1899), 527-535.
37. http://www.uic.edu/depts/hist/hullmaxwell/maxwell/chapters/russheb/section1/documents/twain/CONCJEW.pdf
38. Leo Tolstoy, "What is the Jew?" quoted in The Final Resolution, pg. 189, printed in Jewish World periodical, 1908   http://www.simpletoremember.com/articles/a/quotes/ "When ... I scrutinized the activity of the Jewish people, suddenly there arose up in me the fearful question whether inscrutable Destiny, perhaps for reasons unknown to us poor mortals, did not, with eternal and immutable resolve, desire the final victory of this little nation." Adolf Hitler, Mein Kampf (US, Noontide Press, 2003), p 64. http://www.kabbalah.info/bb/why-do-people-hate-jews/
39. http://www.haaretz.com/jewish/2.209/why-did-adolf-hitler-hate-the-jews-1.2618
40. Blaise Pascal, Pensees, trans. W.F. Trotter, Introduction by T.S. Eliot (Benediction Books, 2011),

41. *http://www.kabbalah.info/bb/why-do-people-hate-jews/ 41 http://www.simpletoremember.com/articles/a/quotes/*
42. *Westerners who study China through its language, literature and history*
43. *http://christiananswers.net/dictionary/miracle.html*
44. *http://www.jpost.com/Israel-News/NGO-Hamas-rocket-attacks-in-2016-lowest-in-11-years-476826*
45. *http://www.inquisitr.com/1364461/israel-miracle-gaza-strip-hamas-complain-their-god-changes-the-paths-of-our-rockets-in-mid-air/*
46. *http://themiracleofisrael.org*
47. *https://www.poets.org/poetsorg/poem/miracles-0*
48. *http://kirkcameron.com/hope-for-our-time-a-christmas-story/*
49. *Letter to John Armstrong, 11 March 1782, in Ford's Writings of George Washington (1891), vol. XII, p. 111. This is frequently attached to part of a letter to Brigadier-General Nelson of 20 August 1778, as in this 1864 example from B. F. Morris, The Christian Life and Character of the Civil Institutions of the United States, pp. 33-34*
50. *http://founders.archives.gov/documents/Washington/05-05-02-0279*
51. *http://www.tourosynagogue.org/history-learning/gw-letter*
52. *http://www.jewishtelegraph.com/enteb_1.html*
53. *http://www.wnd.com/2014/08/israeli-soldier-testifies-to-miracle-in-gaza/*
54. *http://templemountfaithful.org/leadership.php*
55. *http://www.historynet.com/yom-kippur-war-sacrificial-stand-in-the-golan-heights.htm*
56. *https://unitedwithisrael.org/how-one-idf-commander-turned-back-a-syrian-column-in-the-yom-kippur-war/*
57. *http://www.historynet.com/the-war-list-great-tank-commanders.htm*
58. *http://armedforcesmuseum.com/highest-scoring-tank-ace-of-wwii-kurt-knispel/*
59. *http://www.historynet.com/the-war-list-great-tank-commanders.htm*
60. *http://www.timesofisrael.com/senior-infantry-officer-describes-divine-protection-in-gaza/#!*
61. *The bone that supports the tongue, located in the neck between the chin and larynx, which makes human speech possible.*
62. *Can be defined as the highest state of intellectual development and emotional maturity. It is believed that Jesus achieved this [higher state of being] in his human life, and was given this term [Christ] before*

his name as the recognition of his achievement of this spiritual status. This path is open to anyone regardless of their religious tradition if and when he or she is open to become a living vessel of love and truth on the planet and actively strives to attain it. Christ consciousness can also be defined as the state of awareness of our true nature, our higher self, and our birthright as children of God. This philosophy is a major tenant of most religions.

63. *The inner or esoteric dimension of Islam; Sufis surrenders to God, in love, over and over. This involves embracing with love, at each moment, the content of one's consciousness as manifestations of God.*

www.ingramcontent.com/pod-product-compliance
Lightning Source LLC
LaVergne TN
LVHW091548060526
838200LV00036B/756